DEFENDING CHRISTIAN ZIONISM

DEFENDING CHRISTIAN ZIONISM

David Pawson

Anchor Recordings

This edition published in 2013 by
Anchor Recordings Ltd
72 The Street, Kennington, Ashford TN24 9HS UK

For more of David Pawson's teaching,
including MP3s, DVDs and CDs, go to
www.davidpawson.com
For further information, email info@davidpawsonministry.com

ISBN 978 0 9575290 7 6

Printed by Createspace
and
Printed in Great Britain by Imprint Digital, Exeter

Contents

INTRODUCTION

—THE CONTROVERSY

'Zionism' is a comparatively recent word, coined to describe the return of the Jews to the land of their ancestors and the re-establishment of the nation-state of Israel, with Jerusalem (Zion) as their capital. A 'Zionist' is one who takes part in this or supports those who do.

There are Jewish Zionists and Christian Zionists. There are also Jewish anti-Zionists and Christian anti-Zionists. This book is written with the last mentioned group in mind.

JEWISH ZIONISM
This is a movement among Jewish people to re-establish a national home for themselves in their ancient territory in the Middle East, believing it to be the only safe haven from the continual history of anti-Semitic persecution that has been their lot during two millennia of their 'Diaspora' (dispersion among other nations).

Historically, it began with the first groups making '*aliya*' (immigration, a Hebrew word for 'go up' in the last verse in Hebrew scriptures, our 2 Chronicles 36:23), in the last quarter of the nineteenth century under the patronage of Sir Moses Montefiore (whose colony outside Jerusalem is marked by a prominent windmill). The project was crystallised in a manifesto of 1896 entitled 'Der Judenstaat' ('The Jewish

State'), by an Austrian journalist Theodor Herzl, who called the first Zionist Congress in the Basel Casino in Switzerland in 1897 (the assimilated Jews of Germany refused to have it in Munich). There he predicted that the Jewish State would be established in fifty years at the very most (he was two months out).

Another key person was Chaim Weizmann, the Manchester chemist who saved Britain during World War I when running out of ammunition; he successfully produced synthetic acetone from wood pulp. His reward was the 'Balfour Declaration', a letter from the Foreign Secretary giving the approval and backing of the British government, who were to be given the Mandate to govern Palestine in the post-war settlement of the Middle East after liberating it from the Turks.

The appalling attempt to wipe out European Jewry during World War II, known as 'the Holocaust' (in Hebrew *Shoah*, from Isaiah) led directly to David Ben Gurion's declaration of the State of Israel in 1948. In 1967 the old city of Jerusalem (Zion) was recaptured from the Jordanians, completing the hopes of Jewish Zionists and becoming their 'eternal' capital.

JEWISH ANTI-ZIONISM

It may come as a surprise that any Jews would be opposed to the re-establishment of their ancestral homeland, with its offer of a safe refuge for those under pressure elsewhere. But there are, from both ends of the religious spectrum.

At the orthodox end, the belief that Israel can only be properly restored under the reign of the Messiah and must therefore await his return leads to a denial of the present secular democracy as unworthy of the name. This extreme view can be found among Jews living in Jerusalem itself, notably in the orthodox quarter known as the Mea Shearim. They pray for the day when Messiah will legitimise the situation.

At the liberal end, especially among those who do not practise the faith, their objections are political rather than religious. Their desire is to stay where they are, assimilating to the surrounding culture as much as they can. They may support Israel, as a necessary sanctuary for their persecuted relatives, but also see it as a threat to their own security, putting pressure on them to emigrate. They are also aware of the problems facing the infant state, both external and internal, and wish to keep a safe distance away. Conflict in the Middle East affects the whole world and can foster anti-Semitism elsewhere.

So not all Jews welcome Zionism, but those who do not are in a minority.

CHRISTIAN ZIONISM

This is a movement among Gentile believers in the Jewish Messiah to advocate and support the Jewish return to their own land, convinced that they still have a God-given right to be there and, indeed, that he would bring and has brought them home again, thus keeping his promises recorded in the scriptures.

Historically, this began before Jewish Zionism and was initially the result of the Protestant Reformation in northern Europe, which gave the Bible to ordinary people in their own language, encouraging them to interpret it for themselves, instead of the official party line of the medieval church. A fresh appreciation of Israel's past, present and future was inevitable.

Britain could claim to be its birthplace, with two groups as midwives. First were the preachers. In England: the Puritan John Owen, the Wesley brothers, Charles Simeon of Cambridge, Bishop Ryle of Liverpool, the Baptist Charles Haddon Spurgeon. In Scotland: the Presbyterians Andrew Bonar and Murray McCheyne.

Then there were the politicians, laymen well-versed in scripture: Oliver Cromwell, William Wilberforce (who played a leading role in abolishing slavery), Lord Shaftesbury (industrial reformer whose memorial stands in Piccadilly Circus), Lord Palmerston, Earl Balfour (who wrote the famous

'Declaration' assuring the Jewish people of the support of the British Government for a homeland in Palestine), David Lloyd George, Winston Churchill, Harold Wilson (whose large book, *The Chariots of Israel*, revealed his Zionist sympathies). There were prominent military figures, like General Gordon of Khartoum (who 'discovered' Calvary and the Garden tomb), General Allenby (who liberated Jerusalem from the Turks in 1917) and Orde Wingate of Burma (who laid the foundation of the Israeli army, insisting that officers led their troops into battle, as in biblical days).

All these were Christian Zionists, based on their biblical knowledge. Few today are aware of what a major role Britain has played in the rebirth of the State of Israel.

It was the opening of a British consulate in Jerusalem in the middle of the nineteenth century, while the Ottoman Turks occupied desolate and sparsely populated Palestine, that opened the door for Jewish immigrants. Significantly, it shared a compound with the first Protestant church building in the Middle East (Christ Church is still there, just inside the Jaffa Gate), soon to have the first bishop.

One of the major influences on Theodor Herzl was William Hechler, chaplain to the British Embassy in Vienna.

Then, of course, Britain was given the Mandate to govern Palestine by the League of Nations after World War I, making her the last Gentile power to be responsible for the Holy Land. It was the relinquishing of this burden, after violent tensions between Jews and Arabs resulting from incompatible commitments to both, that led directly to Israel's Declaration of political independence.

So Britain as a country, and British Christians, have done more than any other nation to foster Zionism. It is therefore a surprise, to many a shock, that within the same nation has arisen a wave of anti-Zionism, a vociferous — and some would say vicious — attack on Christian Zionists.

CHRISTIAN ANTI-ZIONISM

England has had its own share of anti-Semitism, particularly in the Middle Ages. False accusations of child murder lay behind the building of cathedrals in Lincoln and Norwich. All Jews were banished in 1291. The last Jews in York, besieged in the castle there, did what their forbears had done at Masada, committing suicide rather than be slaughtered by soldiers. During their long absence they were only known by rumoured caricature, as in Shakespeare's *Merchant of Venice*. Not until Cromwell's day were they encouraged to return, for economic reasons, at first illegally but soon legally.

It was the atheistic French Revolution which led to their emancipation in Europe, which in turn led to assimilation which could have meant their elimination in time. But the centuries of religious anti-Semitism ('you killed Jesus so we can kill you') gave way to a racial hatred (as the 'least fittest to survive in the struggle between races'). The rise of nationalism in the early twentieth century led to the worst expression of anti-Semitism in history — the Holocaust. However, there was a direct link from Luther's solution to the 'Jewish problem' and Hitler's.

But is anti-Zionism another variety of anti-Semitism, political rather than religious or racial? Its proponents vehemently protest that it is not. Is it then a complete coincidence that there is a simultaneous rising tide of anti-Semitism in Western civilisation, particularly in Britain and America? We can only say that anti-Zionists need to be extra careful not to be tainted themselves or to exploit in others the hostility towards God's chosen people that seems latent in fallen human nature.

However, we are talking about Christian anti-Zionism in particular, not anti-Semitism in general. Noticeably, this has arisen in Britain following the extraordinary reversal in Israel's fortunes during just one decade in the mid-twentieth century, the 1940s. From being the helpless and hopeless victims of mass extermination they recovered the status of national statehood, players on the world stage influencing all other nations. In spite of a series of wars with her neighbours, Israel has survived against overwhelming odds, ultimately building up the sixth largest army in the world, with nuclear weapons at its disposal.

World sympathy, influenced heavily by the media, has shifted from the Jews to the Arabs, from Israelis to Palestinians. The oppressed are now seen as oppressors. Israel has been accused of 'racism', 'fascism' and 'apartheid' (the last by President Jimmy Carter of the USA). More resolutions have been passed by the United Nations against Israel than any other nation.

Attention has been focused on the plight of Palestinians, both inside and outside Israel's boundaries. Politicians seem to ignore the religious factor (the virulent anti-Semitism of many militant Islamists determined to re-capture Palestine for their god Allah), concentrating on political and humanitarian issues.

The surprising thing is that this swing is reflected in and shared by an increasing number of Christian individuals, churches and organisations (from Christian Aid to the World Council of Churches). Are they just following the opinions of the world, influenced by the spirit of the age?

All Christians know that they should not do this, but have their thinking governed from the inside (Romans 12:2). They need to have godly reasons for their attitudes, another way of saying 'theological justification'. There are four kinds of theology being used to undergird anti-Zionism:

1. Liberal theology. With its assumptions of the universal Fatherhood of God and brotherhood, it is inherently opposed to the divine choice of one nation over against others (scholars call this 'the scandal of particularity'). The 'enlightened' New Testament is thought to have left all that behind.

2. Replacement theology. The international Church has replaced the national Israel as God's people on earth, inheriting

all their promised blessings, but not their curses.

3. Fulfilment theology. Israel was reduced to a 'remnant' of one true Israelite in the person of Jesus. In him all the promises made to the people of Israel were fulfilled and then extended to all who believe in him, whether Jew or Gentile.

4. Liberation theology. Originating among Catholic priests in Latin America and now adopted by many Palestinian Christians, the gospel is seen as good news of freedom from injustice, deprivation and oppression, with a strong emphasis on human rights.

We shall make comments on these throughout the book.

The strongest current wave of anti-Zionism has surfaced among evangelical Christians, noted for their devotion to biblical study. To be more specific, among evangelical Anglican clergy, in sharp contrast to the preachers and politicians of that denomination in previous generations, whom we have already mentioned. Three in particular need to be named.

Colin Chapman put anti-Zionism on the agenda with his book *Whose Promised Land?* (2002). I was invited to discuss it with him on television, but the recorded programme was a disaster and I do not think it was ever broadcast. We had too little in common.

Stephen Sizer has now become the main protagonist. The Vicar of Virginia Water, near Windsor, he was relatively unknown but is now making a name for himself on this issue. He used to be a keen Zionist, even listing myself as an early influence! He has now swung to the opposite extreme. I first met him at a symposium on Israel in London, sponsored by the Evangelical Alliance, but I have since visited him at his home, just up the A30 from me. It was a friendly but unproductive encounter — except that my burden to write this book became heavier.

He has written two books, both published by Inter-Varsity Press, not hitherto associated in my mind with taking strong sides on the subject. The first was a rather academic volume entitled: *Christian Zionism: Road-map to Armageddon?* (2004). A thesis, for which he was awarded a doctorate, provided the basis for that book. IVP requested a more popular version 'for a wider audience' and he produced *Zion's Christian Soldiers? The Bible, Israel and the Church* (2007).

It is this later publication that I am going to address, since it is more likely to be read, with only side references to the former volume, pointing out some quite radical differences between them. One is the omission of a complete section on the 'Political Implications', in which Sizer accuses Christian Zionism of outright militarism, leading to bloodshed, dispossession and division. Is that why both book covers display photographs of armoured vehicles of the Israeli army?

John Stott has made a contribution to both books, in the form of a commendation on the front cover of the first and a previously unpublished sermon in the second. Much more widely known and revered for his many years of biblical preaching, his name undoubtedly adds weight and will ensure a wider readership of Sizer's writings than would otherwise have been the case.

I share the respect and gratitude of many evangelicals for his faithful and consistent expositions of scripture, though we have had our differences of interpretation, notably over the nature of hell, and baptism in the Holy Spirit. However, we share a conviction over male leadership, though our different ecclesiastical affiliations lead us to draw the line at different points. I am saddened that he is making such a public and negative stance on the Zionist question towards the close of such a ministry. (Why was I reminded of Luther's final anti-Semitic outburst?) I have kept my comments on his sermon to an Appendix, since it was not an integral part of the text.

However, Sizer is my main 'target'. His criticisms are expressed in the strongest language, not unlike that of Hamas, who at the time of writing control the Gaza Strip. One of their leaders pronounced that, 'Christian Zionism is the greatest danger to world truth, justice and peace.' Sizer's language in *Christian Zionism* seems to share that opinion.

I am not venturing into the political aspects of the Middle East conflict. It is a minefield (forgive the pun). With rights and wrongs on both sides, it is far too easy to select the facts most congenial to one's sympathies. In any case, Sizer has dropped the extensive political section in his first book from the second more popular version.

However, my main reason for leaving that aspect to others is that for Christians, evangelicals in particular, the biblical question is both fundamental and decisive, whatever the political repercussions. It is a classic case of beliefs affecting attitudes and actions. In addition, I am a Bible teacher rather than a politician and have more experience and a slender claim to expertise in the field of scriptural study.

Every author has to ask why he is writing. The answer defines his reader target and shapes his style. I do not write for scholars but for all interested in the subject and willing to think for themselves. What do I hope to achieve?

Obviously my primary aim is to counter Sizer's case among those who have heard him speak, read his books or simply been aware of his attack. I confess my faith is stretched to believe that Sizer himself will be persuaded to change his mind — again. As an ex-Zionist, who blames me, among others, for misleading him in his earlier position, a reversal would be proof of supernatural intervention! But I hope that many of those who have been impressed by his presentation are still open-minded enough to consider the alternatives objectively and come to their own conclusions.

A secondary aim is to correct the views of some of my fellow Zionists, particularly those of a 'dispensational' viewpoint. They will be disturbed by my agreement with much of Sizer's criticism of this position. I am convinced that association with what I regard as exegetical error is a real handicap to the Zionist cause, preventing its case being heard in many ecclesiastical circles. Until there is a clear disassociation from it, the promotion of Zionism will languish, at least in the United Kingdom, where dispensationalism is widely discredited.

I have also written this book for myself. Writing a book serves to clarify an author's own convictions, even re-thinking some of them. It has also given me an opportunity to present my own position, about which there have been rumours and misunderstanding (Sizer himself classifies me as a dispensationalist!) I need hardly add that I do not speak for anyone else, though I know that many will be glad that I have written.

My first chapter is inevitably negative. In severing any links with dispensational Zionism, I am clearing the site before constructing a positive case for what Sizer used to call 'covenantal' but I now call 'classical' Zionism, based on three of the five covenants in the Bible. We then look at both the people and land of Israel in the light of New Testament data. Finally, we look into the future, helped by New Testament prophecies.

Thank you in advance for your perseverance!

1

TWO ZIONISMS

As already mentioned, Stephen Sizer has written two volumes against Zionism, the first quite 'academic' in style, as befits a PhD thesis, the second for a wider readership and therefore more popular, or at least a bit more readable. There are some differences between the two, perhaps reflecting developments in his thinking.

But there is one huge change in the second which is of major significance.

In the first book he carefully analyses the whole spectrum of Christian Zionism and tabulates the differences between the two major types, labelling them 'covenantal' and 'dispensational'. He further subdivided the latter into three varieties — messianic, apocalyptic and political (see the charts on pp. 256–7). The three sub-divisions are not so clear or so significant as the two main categories, which are the subject of this chapter.

In the second book 'covenantal' Zionism has virtually disappeared from view. One or two stray hints of its existence will be missed by most readers. Instead, his whole assault is directed against 'dispensational' Zionism, as if it is the only form.

To make matters even more confused, he now uses the

label 'covenantal' for his own anti-Zionist stance, leaving the other Zionist position without any identification. Since I belong to and am writing about this viewpoint (now apparently anonymous!), I have chosen to call it 'classical' Zionism, partly because it pre-dated the dispensational and partly because it is the version more characteristic of 'traditional' and 'orthodox' circles (as for most of the preachers and politicians named in the Introduction).

Why has Sizer made this extraordinary shift, transferring a name from one thing to its exact opposite? He does not explain, so we can only speculate. Is it because he and most evangelicals (Anglican and otherwise) belong to the 'Reformed' school of theology (named after the Protestant Reformers, Luther and Calvin), which is also referred to as 'covenant' theology? The term 'covenantal Zionism' could suggest they belong together, which would offend many 'covenant' theologians. They may have complained already about such an unwarranted association.

However, I think it more likely that Sizer is discounting the influence and significance of what he used to call 'covenantal' and I now call 'classical' Zionism. He may be influenced by the numerical factor. Worldwide, 'classicals' are in a minority. The 'dispensationals' are the majority. There is also a geographical factor. Most classicals are in the United Kingdom, most dispensationals in the United States. And Sizer has a particular concern about the latter's effect on American foreign policy in the Middle East.

Or it may simply be that we classicals have spoken and written much less and are therefore not so familiar to the Christian public. It might even be the case that Sizer does not want to publicise our views, which we claim to be both balanced and biblical — not such an easy target for critics!

Sizer's attack is focused on dispensationalists, almost all *across Atlantic* transatlantic. He names Cyrus Scofield (whose annotated Bible has done so much to spread that teaching), Lewis Sperry

Chafer, Jerry Falwell (founder of the 'Moral Majority' lobby), Arnold Fruchtenbaum, Tim LaHaye (whose *Left Behind* series of novels has sold by the millions), Pat Robertson (of the TV *700 Club* and Presidential candidate), Hal Lindsey (whose book *The Late Great Planet Earth* was a worldwide bestseller) and John Hagee (pastor of the Cornerstone Church in San Antonio, Texas and probably the leading Zionist in the USA). Surprisingly, the man behind them all was an Englishman!

John Nelson Darby, named after England's naval hero was an Anglican curate working in Dublin, with a particular concern for the indigenous poor in Ireland. At the beginning of the nineteenth century there was a surge of interest in what the prophetic scriptures had to say about the future, possibly stimulated by the disturbing political events at that time. Conferences of interested Bible students explored the matter. Two such were highly significant, both hosted in mansions, Powerscourt in the Wicklow Mountains south of Dublin (hosted by Lady Powerscourt) and Albury, outside Guildford in Surrey (hosted by Henry Drummond). Darby was an attendee and later founded the movement which became known as 'the Brethren', sometimes called 'the Plymouth Brethren' after one of their major bases. Another attendee was Edward Irving, former minister of the Presbyterian Church of Scotland, subsequently pastor of a thriving church in London and later founder of the now largely defunct Catholic Apostolic Church.

Darby is widely regarded as the originator of the system of biblical interpretation which came to be known as 'dispensationalism'. While some of his ideas had already been mooted by a few individuals, both Catholic and Protestant, he was certainly responsible for bringing them together into a coherent and persuasive framework. And he was also responsible for the wide dissemination of his schematic interpretation of the Bible. His visits to America resulted in the conversion of the lawyer, Scofield, who compiled the Scofield Bible with 'Notes' purveying Darby's views and which became the most popular version among Evangelicals (including the new 'Pentecostals') in America. Dallas Seminary was specifically established on this basis (Hal Lindsey was a student there).

So what are the distinctive doctrines which distinguished 'Darbyism' (as it was nicknamed before it got its label 'dispensationalism') from all other schools of theology? We must begin with a phrase which meant much to Darby and was a root of his thinking, taken from Paul's counselling letters to Timothy. Paul urged his prodigy to be in his preaching and teaching 'a workman who is not ashamed, rightly dividing the word of truth' (2 Timothy 2:15). Darby fastened on the word 'dividing', taking it in its simplest sense of 'cutting up'. Actually, its root refers to ploughing a straight furrow and its application to Bible exposition means opening up the meaning of scripture in a skilful and accurate way (the New International Version helpfully translates the phrase: 'correctly handles'). But Darby took its most literal sense as a key principle and made three fundamental divisions.

1. He divided the biblical history of the world into seven quite distinct periods, called 'dispensations' or 'ages'. In each of these there is a fresh revelation of God's purpose and a new response required from human beings, to which divine grace is 'dispensed' on a developing basis.

Dispensationalists are far from agreed with Darby on when the dispensations begin and end, though all believe there are seven. The first is always God's dealings with innocents Adam and Eve. The sixth and seventh are usually the same, respectively referred to as the 'church age' (from the first coming of Jesus to his second, and mainly Gentile) and the 'kingdom age' (the thousand years of his 'millennial' reign, after his Second Coming and mainly Jewish).

These last two have a profound effect on how the New Testament is understood and applied. In Matthew's Gospel, which is clearly addressed to Jewish readers, the blocks of teaching on the kingdom are referred to the seventh dispensation, making the primary relevance of the Sermon on the Mount (chapters 5–7) ethics for the millennium. The 'signs' of the future (chapters 24–25) are given to the disciples as Jews and are not expected to be seen by Christians. The middle section of the book of Revelation (chapters 6–19) describing the catastrophic climax to the present evil age, the 'great tribulation' or 'big trouble', need not worry Christians because they will have left the world before then, according to the second division Darby made.

2. He divided the Second Coming of Christ into two comings, separated by a number of years. This is probably the most well-known feature of dispensationalism and the readiest method of identifying its devotees.

The first Second Coming is said to be secret, or at least private. The only sign visible to the world will be the sudden absence of all true believers, who will have been caught up to meet the Lord in the air and then taken by him to heaven. Special terms are applied to this event — 'coming for the saints', 'the blessed hope' and, above all 'the rapture' (from the Latin Vulgate version of 1 Thessalonians 4:17, which uses the verb *rapto, raptere* for 'caught up').

A crucial addendum to this notion is that there are no 'signs' preceding this event given in scripture. It could literally happen at any time, any day now, indeed at 'any moment'. This is known as the doctrine of the 'imminent' return of Christ. It is a radical change from the hope of every believer that his second advent will occur in their lifetime.

The second Second Coming will be very public. The whole world will be aware of his presence and of the accompanying crowd of those who had previously disappeared, swelled by all believers in heaven. This is called his coming with his saints, to distinguish it from his former coming for his saints. They will have escaped the terrible distress of the Big Trouble. What will happen to the Jews meanwhile? The answer lies in

Darby's third division.

3. <u>He made a division between Israel and the church</u>. That is, he saw no continuity between the physical people of God (all Jewish) and the spiritual people of God (some Jews but mostly Gentiles). Believing their separateness would extend into eternity, when the Jews would inhabit the new earth and Christians the new heaven, he called them respectively God's 'earthly' and 'heavenly' peoples.

In some ways this sounds similar to 'replacement' theology —that the church has taken the place of Israel. But this is only a temporary state of affairs, in the sixth dispensation, the 'church age'. Dispensationalists seem to teach what I call a 'reverse replacement' or a 'double replacement' theology. As the church has taken over Israel's calling and mission in the present, Israel will take them back again in the future (and, it is implied, complete the task which the church failed to finish!)

This handover will begin at 'the rapture', when the church (and the Holy Spirit, as some interpret 2 Thessalonians 2:7) is removed from the earth. Israel will then take over the task of evangelism during the Big Trouble. They are hardly likely to have much success if the Holy Spirit has left with the church and is no longer around to convict of sin, righteousness and judgement (John 16:8).

However, Israel's full 'restoration' will come in the millennium. Not only will all the land promised to their patriarchs be theirs, from the river of Egypt to the Euphrates, but also the cultus will be restored in Jerusalem, with a rebuilt temple, a recovered priesthood and a revived sacrificial system. The latter will not have any atoning effect, but will be a 'memorial' to Jesus' death, much the same as the Lord's Supper (to comply with the clear teaching in the New Testament, particularly the letter to the Hebrews, which categorically denies their efficacy in the light of Christ's once-for-all sacrifice on the cross).

Ultimately, Israel will occupy the new earth and the new

Jerusalem sent down from heaven for the Jewish people while Christians remain in the new heaven.

Such, in broad outline, is the 'dispensational' scheme of things. As always, there are variations among its adherents and there is a recent development of 'progressive' dispensationalists moving to a more traditional position. But where did it all come from? They would say: from scripture, by taking it literally, as it should be.

But none of the three divisions outlined above can be found stated clearly and simply in the Bible. Not a single text talks about seven dispensations. Not a single text says that Jesus will return twice. Not a single text distinguishes between Jews as God's earthly people and Christians as his heavenly people. So how can they claim these to be biblical divisions?

The answer is by logical deduction from scripture, using inference and implication. But this allows human reason to qualify divine revelation (see my opening remarks in chapter two). It can systematise the Word of God into a doctrinal '-ism', that may be logically consistent within itself but scripturally inadequate and even inaccurate. I regard dispensationalism as one of these and believe it is a misleading system of interpreting scripture, in its three divisions mentioned above and especially the expectation of an 'any-moment' return of the Lord to 'rapture' the saints out of the world before the great tribulation and the eventual public return of Jesus, which is the system's most distinctive feature.

Before we consider the effects of dispensationalism on what we have called classical Zionism, much of which will be seen as negative, let me list some positive results, mainly by way of challenges to the rest of us in the body of Christ.

First, we were challenged to take scripture more literally, which Sizer himself advocates. Protestant Reformers had begun this trend, urging a reading of the Bible according to its plainest, simplest sense unless the text itself indicated otherwise, pointing to a less obvious meaning with symbolical or metaphorical language. But there was one genre of biblical literature which the Reformers continued to interpret allegorically, following the traditional approach of many previous centuries, namely prophecies about the future. And so:

Second, we were challenged to take the predictions in the Old and New Testaments much more seriously. Those made to Israel were to be applied to Israel and only to the church if the New Testament explicitly did so. This was a novel approach at the time and led to:

Third, we were challenged to pay more attention to the Jewish people, still part of God's plans and purposes. The destiny of Israel and the church were interlinked, their access to divine mercy interdependent. This would become increasingly apparent towards the end of the present age. This meant:

Fourth, we were challenged to explore 'eschatology' (from the Greek *eschaton* = end) of scripture. There is a surprising amount of information about events before, during and after our Lord's return to planet earth. There can be an unhealthy curiosity about the future that leads to speculative 'guesstimates' about timing and identification of events and persons, but to dismiss or ignore all this data is equally mistaken. The Lord would not have told us so much unless it was necessary for balanced Christian living. This led to:

Fifth, we were challenged to restore the Second Coming to the central focus of Christian hope for the future. It had tended to slip into a secondary place, unlike the early church and its constant prayer: '*maranatha*' (remembered in its original Aramaic/Syriac form and meaning: 'Lord, come', 1 Corinthians 16:22). In truth, this raised a further issue:

Sixth, we were challenged to re-examine the purpose of his return to earth. Most, if not all, Christians gave lip-service to the fact but few thought about the need or reason for it. Why was he returning? What had he not done on his first visit? How long would he need to stay this time? We shall consider these questions in chapter 5.

All these challenges led to positive gains in the wider church, though they did not necessarily lead to the same conclusions as the dispensationalists had drawn. Overall, the eschatological dimension of the gospel would be recovered, though the 'not yet' aspect of the kingdom could take over from the 'now'. Jesus kept the present and future in perfect balance: his parables of the kingdom are divided exactly 50:50 between the inaugurated and the yet to be consummated kingdom.

It is time to examine the impact of dispensational teaching on Christian Zionism. It has been huge, some would say overwhelming. Certainly this is true in America and, through a record export of evangelical missionaries from that country, is now a worldwide phenomenon.

This was perhaps the inevitable result of the great emphasis on the continuing significance of the Jewish nation in the dispensational scheme. Christians who had previously regarded Jews as a vestigial organ in the body (like the appendix!), of purely historical interest, were now regarding them with new interest, as indicators of what time it was on God's clock, the timetable of the end of the world, making Israel the most relevant nation to watch.

All this indicated a subtle change of emphasis in Christian Zionism which few noticed. Earlier 'classical' Zionism, as I have called it, primarily associated the return of the Jews to the promised land with the past promises of God and only secondarily with his future purposes. Now that would be reversed. The future would predominate. Israel became the precursor of the final countdown of world history.

It went further than that. Since dispensationalism had already decided that all explicit 'signs' of the Lord's return referred to the second part of his return, his public appearance 'with the saints', especially those connected with the great tribulation, the Antichrist and the false prophet, there would therefore be no signs before the first part, his 'imminent' return to earth's atmosphere 'for the saints', to take them up to heaven in 'the rapture'. Sucked into this 'vacuum' (of no signs) has been the return of Israel to her own land, now an established fact. It thus becomes the one and only sign of the 'imminent rapture'.

Naturally, the scriptures have been searched for support of this supposition. While it is true that there are indirect hints that Jerusalem will be in the hands of Jews when Jesus returns (for example, Luke 13:35), there is not a single explicit statement in the New Testament making the Jewish return a 'sign' of Jesus' return. Attempts to find one invariably eisegete (read into) texts, rather than exegete (read out of) them.

Matthew 24:32–34 is a case in point. After giving a clear answer to the disciples' question about 'signs' of his coming by explaining four of them (in the world, in the church, in the Middle East and in the sky), Jesus adds a few general comments intended to encourage them to watch for these signs. The first draws a parallel with their skill in watching for the seasonal signs in nature, at which they are deeply proficient, citing the example of the fig tree's leaves as a sign that summer is coming. He had already drawn a similar moral from red skies at night or in the morning (Matthew 16:2–3). But now what for Jesus was a simple analogy has been turned into an allegory. It is said that because Israel is sometimes said to be like a fig tree elsewhere in scripture (which is true), that must also be the case here. The fig tree budding must be the rebirth of the State of Israel! But this does not logically follow. Israel is also likened to a vine, but that does not mean that every other mention of a vine is a reference to the nation of Israel. In any case, Luke's record of this very same statement includes the sprouting leaves of 'the fig tree and all the trees' (Luke 21:29, pointing to a general analogy, not a particular allegory).

Once verse 32 is taken as an allegory of Israel, the next two verses are distorted in meaning and application. 'Even so', which clearly indicates a simple analogy, 'when you

26

see all these things', a reference assumed to refer to Israel's return, rather than the four major developments previously listed — which leads on to 'this generation will certainly not pass away' which was taken to mean the generation that was living in 1948. It has added up to a feverish expectation of Jesus' return in our lifetime. The chief Rabbinate has recently accused Christian Zionists of loving Israelis not so much for themselves but as a 'sign' of the end times. My version is to ask if Jesus does not return for another hundred years, what will happen to your attention to and affection for Israel? Would disappointment lead to disinterest?

Dispensational Zionists can be accused of introducing a note of insincerity into their vociferous support of Israel. While vehemently assuring Israelis of their constant alliance and advocacy, they are inwardly expecting to be 'taken up' out of this world any day now, leaving Israel alone in this world to face the biggest troubles of all. Some might call this hypocrisy.

As well as these direct effects of their 'rapture' belief, there are other indirect influences. From observation and experience, I have concluded that dispensationalists are particularly prone to weaknesses which can affect any Zionists. I refer to the following tendencies, or should I call them temptations?

1. To seek to 'comfort' Jewish people rather than convert them ('convert' in the sense of bringing them to saving faith in their own Messiah, rather than incorporating them into Gentile Christianity). It may be that the combination of Jesus returning any time now and the promise that 'all Israel will be saved' then if not before has encouraged people to think there is little point in trying to save them now. Or it may be that the frenetic desire to befriend Israel has become such a priority that it must not be risked by the offence of the gospel. Some organisations supporting immigration to Israel even expect an undertaking never to try and evangelise those they assist. Whatever, it seems strange for a Christian to profess love for anyone without wanting to see them saved. Paul would never

have approved of that (Romans 9:3; 10:1; 11:14). It goes without saying that we have to earn the right to preach to Jews, overcoming the suspicion of centuries, often by demonstrating unfeigned love in practical ways, but to stop short of seeking their actual salvation would seem a failure in Christian love.

An extreme version of this is to so emphasise respect for and tolerance of Judaism that it is accepted that Jews don't need salvation. This is known as the 'dual covenant' theory. Jews are saved by the 'old' covenants and the Christians by the 'new' (see chapter 2 about this). Dialogue replaces evangelism.

After the Holocaust and in the light of contemporary world opinion, Israel certainly needs comfort but, like all other nations, needs salvation even more.

2. To support Israel right or wrong, or even to think Israel can do no wrong. But the government of Israel is not infallible and the soldiers in her army are capable of blunders. Over-eagerness to support Israel can blind the eyes to political and military mistakes. Perhaps this is a reaction to the tendency in the world and particularly the media to judge Israeli 'atrocities' by a stricter standard than Arab outrages, one seen as the brutality of an occupying power and the other as the only option for 'freedom fighters'.

There are wrongs on both sides of the Middle East conflict and it is too easy to take sides. Christians should be as objective and impartial in their judgements as the God they love and worship. The problem is that he knows all the facts while we, dependent so largely on a mixture of personal experience and public media, rarely see the whole picture. We should therefore be hesitant to apportion blame or to back purely political solutions, much less military actions. We also need to give careful consideration before jumping to conclusions that specific acts are unjust or immoral, in a climate where observers are only too ready to express such opinions — about everyone but themselves!

3. To see the Middle East conflict solely in religious terms.

While politicians seem to ignore the religious dimension, namely the hostility between Islam and Judaism, the hatred of Muslims for Jews, Christians can go to the other extreme, blind to the humanitarian fall-out and deaf to Palestinian pleas for justice. We cannot be indifferent to human suffering at ground level, whoever is causing it. (Ordinary citizens of Gaza suffer as much from their new government as they ever did from former Israeli occupation and present Israeli retaliatory raids). Any state of war involves civilian hardships and casualties, however hard the belligerents try to avoid them.

That there are underlying spiritual forces at work should be obvious to any who believe in the demonic dimension to the struggle between good and evil, the existence of 'principalities and powers' above and beyond human conflicts (Ephesians 6:12). That realisation should motivate us to more appropriate strategy and tactics of defence and attack than mere political or military action, which can never solve the real situation.

That Islam is now a far greater threat to Christianity than communism ever was and even secularism now is (given that even fallen human nature still has a 'God-shaped blank' to fill with someone or something) should go without saying. This peril is now world-wide. Yet church leaders are increasingly expressing sympathy and forging alliances with Muslim leaders, on the mistaken assumption that monotheistic religions have enough in common to stand together. (See my book: *The Challenge of Islam to Christians*).

Nevertheless, it is still wrong to see this as the only factor preventing peace. Zionists should know their prophetic scriptures better than that.

4. To ignore believers in the region, both Israelis and Arab, or even to be completely unaware of their existence. Christian 'pilgrims' to the Holy Land often go and come back without having met even one. Zionists can have their own version of this neglect.

They can attend conferences and celebrations in Jerusalem,

taking part in marches of witness before thousands of unbelieving Israelis and still have little or no contact with indigenous believers. In its earlier years the International Christian Embassy could have been accused of shunning them, over-anxious to avoid any appearance of being a missionary organisation. Under the present leadership that has radically changed.

There are tens of thousands of believers within the borders of Israel, both Arab and Israeli, and mixed meetings of the two, in hundreds (though these have to be discreet, for obvious reasons).

And then there are the Palestinian believers, though these are a diminishing number, many escaping from Muslim opposition and Israeli irritation to the West (Bethlehem has ceased to be a 'Christian' town). And they are deeply divided themselves between Zionistic sympathies (in Brethren, Pentecostal and independent fellowships) and strongly held anti-Zionist attitudes (in older mainline denominations like Anglican, Catholic and Orthodox).

All of these are brothers and sisters in Christ, all are under real pressure and all need and deserve our sympathy and support.

Other weaknesses to which Zionists, and dispensational Zionists in particular, are subject could be listed: for example, a reluctance to engage in any social or political action, except on behalf of Israel. But enough has been said to demonstrate that there are real risks associated with their position, of which some are more aware than others.

Insofar as there is any truth in the charges made against them, I hope that all Zionists reading this will recognise it and resolve to correct their attitudes and actions. I only ask that anti-Zionists will do the same with the errors exposed in later chapters.

Meanwhile, I am grateful to Stephen Sizer for drawing attention to the legitimate criticisms of dispensational Zionism.

He has rendered a service to the cause of Zionism which was needed. I am among those who are convinced that the case for Zionism will never commend itself more widely to the British Church until its association with dispensationalism is firmly and publicly severed.

But Sizer is very mistaken to lump Zionism and dispensationalism together, as he appears to do in his second volume, leaving his readers with no other choice than to accept or reject both. Hopefully, this chapter has opened up a third possibility — of seeing and considering them separately.

The rest of this book is devoted to Sizer's erroneous notions about what I have called 'classical' Zionism, chief of which is his failure to distinguish the different covenants of the Bible, by no means confined to anti-Zionists but which lies at the heart of their case. To this we now turn.

2

FIVE COVENANTS

Why are there such deep differences among evangelical Bible teachers, all of whom believe in the inspiration and authority of the scriptures? To put the question another way, how can they read the same text, yet come up with such a variety of interpretations and applications? The answer is twofold.

First, they are using different methods. We have already looked at one example in the previous chapter. Some use scripture inductively, building only on what is explicit, what is clearly stated. We call this 'exegesis' (from the Greek word *ex* = out), bringing out of the text what is obviously there, easily seen by any reader. Others use scripture deductively, building on what they believe is implicit, what may be logically deduced or inferred. The danger of this approach is that revelation has been supplemented by reason, which can lead to 'eisegesis' (from the Greek word *eis* = into), reading into the text what is not obviously there, not easily seen by any reader, until they are taught to find it.

Second, they are bringing different presuppositions. We can all make assumptions before we study scripture, which influence what we expect to find there — and what we don't expect to see. We can come with pre-judgement (the meaning of prejudice!) about what the text ought to say, rather than with an open mind ready to accept what it actually does say. Many factors are behind this complication, from tradition to temperaments. But the most common is the prior adoption of what is called a 'systematic theology', usually based on the deductive method already mentioned. These try to fit the whole Bible into a consistent framework of thinking, seen as a key to unlock its message. Such systems are usually identified by a label ending in '-ism', such as 'Calvinism' and 'Arminianism'. In Sizer's book he pits his own 'covenantism' against 'dispensationalism'. All such are left with 'problem passages', texts which don't easily fit into the system!

Bible students and teachers need to become aware of their own prejudices and presuppositions, recognising them for what they are and refusing to allow them to interfere with their understanding of God's Word. But intellectually as well as morally, it is easier to notice the splinter blurring someone else's vision than the joist blocking one's own! The objective must always be to let the Bible speak for itself, to discover its original meaning before applying it to the here and now — what the writer wanted to say, how his readers would have understood it and, above all, what the Holy Spirit intended to communicate.

Probably the most crucial and fundamental question of all biblical interpretation is this: how do the two Testaments, Old and New, relate to each other? Is there a basic continuity between them or a basic discontinuity? Or is there a combination of both? And if so, how do we distinguish between them?

The very different answers to that last question among evangelicals today lie behind the current controversy over the nation of Israel, as with many other issues. They can be identified by a simple criterion: how the word 'covenant' is used.

The Bible, alone among all 'sacred' scriptures, speaks of a covenant-making God. To say that this is astounding would be an understatement! That the maker of the entire universe should even be aware of our existence on this tiny speck of interstellar dust, let alone want to have a personal relationship with us, is amazing. That he, to whom the nations are a drop of water in a bucket, should voluntarily put himself under binding obligation to any of us, is a wonder worthy of worship.

He is also a covenant-keeping God. His character prevents him from even saying what he does not mean, telling a lie or breaking a promise (that alone is enough to convince us we are sinners needing his forgiveness!) 'I will' is not only the most important phrase in the solemnising of marriage: it is the most frequent phrase on God's lips throughout the whole Bible, always in connection with a covenant.

So how many covenants are there in the Bible? Answers reveal immediately which school of interpretation or systematic theology is influencing an approach to scripture.

ONE

'Reformed' theology, based on the Protestant reformers Luther and Calvin, is alternatively called 'covenant' theology because of its emphasis on 'the covenant of grace', that is a single covenant embracing the whole of scripture and all God's dealings with human beings. The idea itself cannot be found anywhere in scripture, but is a simple device to emphasise the truth that all God's initiatives towards us are motivated by his grace, his undeserved favour, regardless of anything we have done or not done. Some covenantists add a second 'covenant of works', but limit this to the brief spell of Adam's innocence when his relationship with God depended on his obedience to the divine prohibition of fruit from the tree of knowledge. But this is irrelevant subsequent to the Fall, so for all practical purposes, the one 'covenant of grace' covers the rest of holy history.

This view leads to a strong emphasis on continuity between the Testaments. A single covenant means that God only has one people on earth, those who have been chosen according to grace. 'Israel' can be called the 'church' of the Old Testament, and the 'church' can be called the 'Israel' of the New. The names are interchangeable, because both were phases in the life of one people, even though one was basically Jewish and the other largely Gentile. There are many implications of this identification at a practical level. Sunday is the equivalent of the Sabbath. Infant baptism is the equivalent of circumcision. Holy Communion is the equivalent of the Passover. And so on.

I suspect that Sizer is at heart a one covenant man, as most evangelical Anglicans have to be, subscribing to the Reformed theology of the Thirty-nine Articles. He calls himself a 'covenantist', and he occasionally slips in the phrase 'the covenant of grace'. But in his attack on Zionists he bases his tactics on an assumption of two covenants, respectively the 'old' and 'new', emphasising the discontinuity between them.

TWO
This is possibly the most widespread answer to how many covenants God has made. It has been fostered in the minds of many, even subconsciously, by the misleading titles given to the two sections of our Bibles. (I don't know who first thought of the two titles, but I cannot believe they were inspired by the Holy Spirit, any more than I can accept that God intended the books of the Bible to be carved up into numbered chapters and verses!) 'Testament' is most confusing because it is a synonym of 'covenant', thus conveying the notion that God made only two.

Sizer argues from this assumption and its corollary that in this matter, as in every other, 'new' replaces 'old'. This lies at the heart of what is called 'replacement' theology, the idea that the church has replaced Israel in God's actions and even his affections. He lumps together all God's dealings with Israel as 'old covenant', which is now obsolete, aged and will soon disappear (Hebrews 8:13). The 'new' covenant has created a new people, no longer defined by physical descent from Abraham, but by spiritual assent to Jesus, not in any way related to ethnic origin but reproduced by evangelistic outreach. Promises of a physical land to an ethnic group are now at best an irrelevance and at worst a theological heresy and a political danger. Zionists are thought to be abandoning the 'new' covenant/Testament and returning to the 'old' covenant/Testament.

FIVE

Actually, the Bible describes five distinct covenants which God made over the centuries with people on earth. They are usually named after the person initially involved, hence referred to as the Noahic, Abrahamic, Mosaic, Davidic and Messianic covenants. There are two important facts about all of them, which should be noted before looking at each of them.

First, all five of them can be found in the Old Testament, and all five of them are also to be found in the New Testament! They are not split between them, which may come as a surprise to some readers.

Second, even more significant, only one of the five is called 'the old covenant' — the 'Mosaic'. And only one of them is called 'the new covenant' — the 'Messianic'. It is only in the case of these two that one has superseded the other. The other three continue to be relevant in the New Testament.

With these two vital facts firmly fixed in our minds we can now look at each of them in detail.

1. NOAHIC

This was established with Noah immediately after the flood

subsided and was the only covenant God ever made with the whole human race. He promised never to use that remedy for human depravity again, adding a positive promise to maintain the cycle of seasons in nature as long as the earth existed, thus ensuring the means of survival for all humans for all time. Production of food depends on light and moisture. When both come together, sun and rain, a coloured ring, the rainbow, appears and acts as a reminder, to God himself rather than to us, of his self-imposed obligation.

In return, he expected us to regard human life as sacred and murder as sacrilege, to be punished by execution. Though animals could now be killed for meat, it must be done humanely, and not be consumed while the life-blood remained in any part. However, the covenant was not conditional on this respect for life — or I would not be here to write this, nor you to read it! God has kept his promise.

2. ABRAHAMIC

Some have called this the most important covenant of all five. It is the one on which all later ones are based. It marks the inauguration of God's rescue of the human race from itself, the opening chapter of the story of our redemption, beginning with just one elderly man.

It was made with Abraham after he had uniquely trusted the only God there is by leaving his comfortable, brick-built home (I kid you not) to live in a tent for the rest of his old age, trekking hundreds of miles to settle in a range of mountains he had never seen or even heard of.

This single individual was to change the course of history for ever. Millions of people are in debt to him, even to this day. Whole nations have been influenced. Western civilisation can trace its origins to him. His life, or at least the latter part of it, was of epic significance. Yet he was far from perfect. He could tell lies to save his own skin as well as anyone. What marked him out was his faith, that trust in and obedience to God, which is counted to be the most fundamental characteristic of a good man in God's sight, the foundation of all other virtues and achievements.

God promised to bless him and his descendants, who would be as numerous as sand on the seashore and stars in the sky, even though his wife was years past fertility. And he would give them, as a possession for all time, the land he had brought them to. Abraham lived to see a son born to his aged wife, but by the time he died he only owned by purchase a tiny patch of land, in which he had buried her. Yet he 'left' the whole country to his son Isaac, who in turn left it to his grandson Jacob (later called 'Israel'), whose twelve sons would become twelve tribes and then a nation. God repeated and renewed the covenant with the son and the grandson, even taking their names into his own! For ever afterwards he would be known as the 'God of Abraham, Isaac and Jacob', the fathers or 'patriarchs' of the nation of Israel.

This covenant had international as well as national promises. This family of three generations would channel benefits to all other families on earth. But they could mediate harm as well as good, depending on the attitude of others. Those who blessed this people (with helpful words and deeds) would enjoy a divine blessing. Those who cursed them (with hurtful words and deeds) would suffer a divine curse. The way God's people on earth are treated matters greatly to God in heaven; hurt them and he is hurt — and will in turn hurt those who hurt them. He is a just and jealous God.

This covenant is full of 'I will' promises (count them in Genesis 12–17), but there are no 'you shall' or 'you shall not' commandments given with them. It is an unconditional offer without demands. The only thing required of Abraham's descendants to qualify for the benefits is that they carry in their bodies the identification mark of circumcision, that surgical operation on the reproductive organ which links them to their forefather, usually visible only to God (Genesis 17:14).

3. MOSAIC

The covenant made at Sinai was, like the Abrahamic, made after the children of Israel had left the land in which they had been living, latterly as slaves. They also had left in obedience, but this time their trek to the promised land was only made possible by the miraculous interventions of God himself. Humanly speaking, their escape from Egypt was impossible. They would remember their 'redemption' every year for ever after in the feast of Passover.

The first thing to notice is that this covenant was concerned with their occupation of the promised land. Its ownership had already been settled a few hundred years before with the patriarchs. This was an additional covenant which did nothing to modify the previous one. It would be the nearest Israel ever had to a national constitution and gave them an extensive body of legislation, anticipating many of the situations they would encounter when they reached their destination.

Embodied in the five books of Moses, Genesis to Deuteronomy, called the 'Torah' (which means 'instruction') most of it is given to 'laws', both major (the Ten Commandments) and minor (six hundred and three others). Covering every aspect of life (diet to dress, marriage to murder, work to worship), it needs to be noted that there are more negatives ('thou shalt not') than positives ('thou shalt').

All this points to the most obvious and significant contrast between the Abrahamic and the Mosaic covenants. The former was virtually unconditional (many 'I will' promises with only one 'you must' requirement relating to the 'sign' of circumcision), and the latter very conditional (few 'I will' promises with many 'you must' requirements). This time the people's response 'we will' was all-important (Exodus 19:7–8). Putting it another way, this covenant is full of the phrase 'if you' followed by 'then I'. The covenant is conditional through and through.

Another feature is the multiplicity of sanctions, blessings and curses, rewards and punishments, all depending on whether the people 'keep' the covenant and fulfil their obligations, which they had readily, perhaps rashly, promised to do ('do' is another key word, used frequently). The punishments ranged from restitution to execution for individual disobedience; and through natural disasters and enemy occupation to forced exile at the national level.

4. DAVIDIC

The only covenant to be made with one person, the promise was a perpetual dynasty to succeed King David, the man 'after God's own heart' who ruled the kingdom of Israel at its peak. His immediate successors would reign on a conditional basis, depending on their walk before the Lord. But there would be one ultimate successor who would occupy the throne permanently. He would, of course, be a physical descendant, a 'son' of David from the same 'root of Jesse', David's father.

5. MESSIANIC

Like the Davidic, this covenant was announced but not achieved in the Old Testament era. Three 'major' prophets each made their own contribution towards what was to come.

Jeremiah revealed WHAT would be its unique features. Promised to the houses of Israel and Judah, the now divided nation with ten tribes in the north and two in the south, this 'new' covenant would contrast with that of Sinai in two ways. First, it would be *internal*, the human obligations written in hearts rather than on stone. Second, it would be *individual*, dealing with 'each' rather than all.

God's offer was threefold. He would give an *inclination* towards keeping his laws rather than a rebellion against them; an *intimacy* with himself, rather than through indirect instruction; and an *innocence* based on complete forgiveness, in place of the inhibition of guilt.

All this was designed to help Israelites maintain their side of the covenant, which so far they had spectacularly failed to do. God was telling them he would not only be faithful to his obligations but would also help them to keep theirs.

Ezekiel revealed HOW this would be achieved. On the one hand, the *human spirit* would be renewed, so that it became softer and more sensitive. On the other hand, the *divine Spirit* of God himself would be received, so that his power and purity would be released. The combination of these two changes would transform the human weaknesses which had been exposed by the Mosaic covenant.

Isaiah revealed WHO would bring it about. The Davidic covenant is here linked with this 'new' covenant in a promised 'anointed' one (in Hebrew *Mashiach*, in Greek *Christos*, in English 'Christ'). He would be the *supreme sovereign* over Israel and indeed all the nations; but he would also have to be the *suffering servant*, paying the penalty for their sins with a painful and humiliating death before being raised from the dead.

Of course it is only in hindsight that we can see how the predictions of these three prophets come together in a glorious covenant, both the final and the finest of all five. With it God will have done all that is needed to save ourselves and our environment from disaster. He will do no more. The rest depends on our response to the initiatives he has taken in making such self-imposed promises and obligations.

It is time to turn to the New Testament and see what is said there about all five covenants. All five are mentioned, directly or indirectly, with some surprising conclusions. It will be easier and probably more helpful to study them in a rather different order than the one we used with the Old Testament.

MESSIANIC ('new')
It is hardly surprising to find that the portion of scripture we call the 'New Testament' majors on the 'new' covenant. As already

noted, the words are synonymous. But the understanding of it is developed in three vital directions.

First, only announced in the Old Testament, it has now been activated. In his death, resurrection and ascension, Jesus, the Son of Man and the Son of God, has done all that was needed to make the promises possible. Sins can now be forgiven and the Spirit poured out from heaven. This is the heart of the gospel, the 'good news' to be proclaimed worldwide.

Second, though it is made available to all, it will only become effective when it is accepted by any. In fact, it is a conditional covenant, depending on the continued repentance and faith of its recipients. It is an offer of salvation, freedom from the penalty of sin (justification), the power of sin (sanctification) and the presence of sin (glorification), but only to the penitent faithful.

Third, it is truly international. The inclusion of Gentile nations was not entirely novel. At least two of the covenants with Israel contained international elements, the Abrahamic and the Davidic. Though this new covenant was offered 'first' to the Jews by Jesus himself (Matthew 10:5 – 6) and later by the apostles (Romans 1:16), it was quickly extended to the Gentiles, as Jewish prophets had predicted (Romans 9:25 –26, quoting Hosea 2:23 and 1:10). While the new covenant community has always included some Jews, it now includes many, many more Gentiles. However, God has planned and promised that one day it will embrace many more Jews (Romans 11:26).

The very word 'new' implies that it follows and replaces the 'old'. Predictably, the New Testament draws attention to this contrast, in many passages in both Gospels and Epistles.

But the key question is: which of the five covenants is the 'old' one? A careful study of all the relevant texts leads to a clear and simple answer.

MOSAIC

Jeremiah himself had said this when predicting the new covenant: 'It will not be like the covenant I made with their forefathers when I took them by the hand to lead them out of the land of Egypt . . . .' (Jeremiah 31:32), a clear reference to their ancestors in the book of Exodus rather than the patriarchs in Genesis, the Mosaic rather than the Abrahamic covenant.

One book in the New Testament which majors on the contrast between 'old' and 'new' is the anonymous letter to the Hebrews. The former is declared to be obsolete and 'what is obsolete and ageing will soon disappear' (8:13). The writer's clear intention is to persuade Jewish believers in Jesus not to revert to Judaism. The pressure to do so was safety for themselves and their families. Christianity was an illegal religion and persecution had already begun (vandalism, assault and imprisonment but not yet martyrdom), whereas Rome had recognised Judaism and synagogues were safe. But returning there involved public denial that Jesus was the Messiah (Christ).

The writer uses every persuasive device, from heartfelt appeals to severe warnings. However, his main argument is that they will be leaving a 'better' faith for a far more inferior one, leaving substance for shadows, anti type for types, heavenly realities for earthly reflections, a transforming relationship with the Son of God for the veneration of the servants of God, whether angelic or human.

What is highly significant is that everything this author dismisses as ineffective, irrelevant and even injurious for the Jewish believers in Jesus is found in the Mosaic covenant and not in any of the others. Surprisingly, he calls it the 'first' covenant, though historically it was the second with Israel, centuries after the first with Abraham. But for Judaism, then as now, the Mosaic, embodied in the Torah, clearly takes first place, dominating their belief and behaviour.

By contrast, this letter contains the strongest affirmation of the Abrahamic covenant in the entire New Testament (which we shall look at shortly). It could not be clearer that 'old' did not include all the covenants made with Israel in the period covered by the Old Testament. Two other features of the New Testament are relevant to our discussion.

One is Paul's teaching about the Mosaic. Not only was it a (much) later addition to the Abrahamic, altering none of its provisions. It was a temporary addition, in contrast to the permanent character of its predecessor. It was a vital element to prepare the people of Israel to receive their Messiah, after which it would become outmoded (Galatians 3:19).

The other is the major controversy of the early church over circumcision. While it was a sign of the Abrahamic covenant, the debate centred on the Mosaic. Paul never criticised continuing this practice among Abraham's descendants from his flesh (a point many overlook). He even advocated it for evangelists working among Jews (Acts 16:3). But he fought long and hard for the freedom of his Gentile converts from being Judaised by pressure to submit to this rite. They were Abraham's children by faith, inheriting the blessing promised to all families on earth. Why was Paul so adamant, then, in opposing this Abrahamic 'sign'? It was not because baptism had superseded it (no-one even thought of saying this). It was because it would tie them in to the Mosaic covenant (Galatians 5:3). Above all, it would rob the 'new' covenant of its universal scope, making it a national, even ethnic, promise, requiring identification with Abraham in flesh as well as in faith.

The general New Testament emphasis on believers not being 'under law' and being 'free from the law' clearly refer to Mosaic legislation. This is a mixture of ceremonial, civil and moral edicts, suited to a theocratic state concerned with all three. But the law is an integrated whole, its elements so mutually interdependent that to transgress any part is to break the whole (Matthew 5:19; Galatians 3:10; James 2:10).

It has been a constant temptation for the church to put

Christians back under the Mosaic covenant. In the early days this may have been due to the fact that the Old Testament canon (rule) was complete and was used as their first 'scriptures'; the New Testament canon took time to assess, assemble and approve. It is often the result of applying both Testaments indiscriminately, without discerning the covenantal framework of its requirements.

Take the widespread division between priest and people, clergy and laity, professional and amateur ministry — straight out of the 'old' covenant. Add altars, vestments and incense and the culture of tabernacle and temple is being revived. At the opposite end of the denominational spectrum, tithes and offerings are mandatory, including the blessing attending the practice (Malachi 3:10), but omitting the curse on failure (Malachi 3:9), though both belong to the 'old'. In the 'new' God only accepts what people want to give (2 Corinthians 9:7), motivated by gratitude for grace received.

But what about the 'Ten Commandments', often adorning church walls alongside the Lord's Prayer and the Apostles' Creed? Surely that bit of the 'old' survives into the 'new', even if the rest of the Mosaic legislation is discarded?

Let it be stated straight away that the new covenant is not without law. Some have so emphasised free grace that they fall into the error of 'antinomianism' (lawlessness, based on the Greek word *nomos* = law). Partners in the new covenant are under the law of Christ, not the law of Moses. Putting it another way, they are subject to Jesus' re-interpretation of the latter. He re-affirms nine of the Ten Commandments, giving the sixth and seventh (murder and adultery) a much stricter application to inward attitude as well as outward action. Gentile believers are free to choose whether to observe the fourth (Sabbath) or not (Romans 14:5) and are warned about the dangers of doing so (Colossians 2:16)! Above all, the love shed abroad in new covenant hearts by the Holy Spirit given to them (Romans 5:5) will fulfil the law without needing to be told (Romans 13:10), which is precisely what Jeremiah meant (31:33).

We have said more than enough to show that the Mosaic covenant is both annulled and fulfilled in the Messianic. It is no longer a necessary component in the relationship between God and his people. The 'new' has superseded the 'old'. This is the truly biblical 'replacement theology'. However, it does not follow that a 'new covenant people', the church, have replaced the 'old covenant people', Israel. That would only be the case if all the covenants of the Old Testament were dismissed as 'old', which is simply not the case. There are three remaining. What does the New Testament make of them?

NOAHIC

I do not know of anyone who has seriously claimed that this has been superseded by the new covenant. The fact that we are still here is enough to confirm its permanent validity. Jesus virtually confirmed it in the Sermon on the Mount when he pointed out that our Father in heaven causes his sun to rise on the evil and the good, and sends rain on the righteous and the unrighteous (Matthew 5:45), indicating an unconditional covenant independent of human behaviour. When sun and rain come together, a rainbow results, reminding God rather than us of his self-imposed obligation.

However, this covenant was unique, the only one made with the whole human race. What about the other two covenants in the Old Testament, both relating to the people of Israel?

ABRAHAMIC

Abraham figures prominently in the New Testament. His name appears nearly fifty times. Both Matthew and Luke include him in the genealogy of Jesus, though Matthew, writing for Jewish readers, stops there, while Luke, writing for a Gentile, takes the family tree back to Adam, emphasising his common roots with humanity.

Right at the beginning of the Gospel story, in what scholars call 'the birth narratives', we find Mary, the mother of Jesus, and Zechariah, the father of John, both praising God for 'remembering his covenant' with Abraham (Luke 1:54–55, 72–73). This is the exact same language used when God intervened to rescue his people from slavery in Egypt (Exodus 2:24) and signals a second 'redemption' of his people Israel, this time from their sins (note 'his people' in the meaning of the name 'Jesus', in Hebrew 'Yeshua' (Matthew 1:21).

Jesus made some striking references to Abraham during his public ministry. He claimed that he was still alive (Mark 12:27); that they were contemporaries in touch with each other, during both their lives on earth (John 8:56–58). Quite simply, if the new covenant Jesus would establish by his death (Luke 22:20) annulled or even altered in any way the Abrahamic, Jesus could and should have informed Abraham of the change. There is no record of him having done so or even needing to.

We have already noted the dual aspect of that covenant made two millennia previously, benefiting both his descendants who shared his (circumcised) flesh and his worldwide children who shared his faith. It is not surprising that the New Testament focuses on the latter 'offspring'. The covenant promises had included God's intention to make him 'the father of many nations' (Genesis 15:5; 17:5, quoted in Romans 4:17–18). In a real sense, he would inherit 'the world' (Romans 4:13).

It is a major mistake to assume that the emphasis on the international aspect has excluded the national. It is a classic case of 'both-and', rather than 'either-or'. Abraham is both the father of one (Jewish) nation and many (Gentile) nations. But for the credited righteousness which brings salvation, both the one and the many need to share Abraham's faith 'fully persuaded that God had power to do what he promised' (Romans 4:21; the whole chapter needs to be read very carefully).

For Paul 'Israel' remained as a unique ethnic group in God's sight, as we shall see in the next chapter. They will always be 'beloved on account of the patriarchs' (Romans 11:28), with whom that foundational covenant had been made. Their benefits from it were as 'irrevocable' as the promises of God (11:29).

No writer of the New Testament brings out the permanent validity of the whole Abrahamic covenant so clearly or emphatically as the anonymous author of the epistle to the Hebrews, the very letter which declares the Mosaic covenant obsolete! In a crucial passage (6:13–18), he points to the solemnising of the covenant promises with a binding oath. Men swear by someone greater than themselves, calling on such to kill them if they are lying or later break a promise, going back on their word. The usual oath is: 'By God, I will . . . .' Since there is no-one greater than God for God to call on as witness, he has to swear by himself: 'By myself, I have sworn.' Such divine oaths are not frequent in scripture and all the more impressive for their rarity.

The fact is that God, by his very character, is incapable of telling a lie, so any statement he makes is absolutely true and utterly reliable, even without swearing to it. He only adds an oath to impress those to whom he is speaking that he really means what he says. (Christians are forbidden to swear at all, but simply tell the truth and be trusted to do so; Matthew 5:33–37.) In the case of his oath to Abraham, 'God wanted to make the unchanging nature of his purpose very clear to the heirs of what was promised' (6:17, NIV). Note the word 'unchanging'.

The writer goes on to point out the implications for his readers and puts it very simply. It is precisely because God has affirmed and consistently applied his promises to Abraham that they, and we today, can trust his promises completely and put our hope for the future in his word. Putting that negatively, if he reneged on any of his covenant with Abraham, we could never be sure that the new covenant is any more trustworthy.

To question one would be to shake the other. Those who claim that any part of God's covenant with Abraham has been changed (for example, that 'a land' has become 'the world') need to be warned that they are undermining the confidence of Christian believers.

DAVIDIC

The name 'David' occurs forty times in the New Testament, frequently as part of one of Jesus' titles: 'Son of David'. Sure enough, the genealogies of Matthew and Luke point out this royal descent from Israel's supreme monarch. (Matthew makes the point in a subtle way by dividing the family tree into three sections of fourteen generations, fourteen being the numerical value of the Hebrew letters of David's name, the letters being used as numbers, then, as in A=1, B=2, C=3, etc.)

'King of the Jews' was another title given to Jesus at his birth (Matthew 2:2), as it would be at his death (John 19:19). There is a very significant item in the birth narratives as well. When the angel Gabriel made his astounding announcement to Mary in Nazareth, about her virginal conception of the Son of the Most High, he added a promise that, 'The Lord God will give him the throne of his father David, and he will reign over the house of Jacob for ever' (Luke 1:32–33, NIV). David's throne was on earth, in Jerusalem, and it was over one nation, Israel. Did Gabriel get his wires crossed? Was this a false message, soon to be shown as out-of-date and misleading? That is implied by those who claim that Jesus never intended to do any such thing, that he came to bring a spiritual kingdom, not a political one.

Throughout his public ministry, the needy called on Jesus as 'Son of David', revealing their belief that he was the Messianic king they had been expecting for a very long time. They hoped he would restore their nation to the glories of the past. The welcome, when he rode into Jerusalem, with cries of *Hoshana* ('Save us now'), raised their hope to a peak, only to be dashed to the ground within a matter of days, when he was executed as a common criminal and buried out of sight. Few more poignant cries have been uttered than 'we had hoped that he was the one who was going to redeem Israel' (Luke 24:21, NIV). Their disappointment was not just in Jesus. It was in God himself, whose promises through the prophets seemed to be postponed indefinitely.

The resurrection changed all that. Triumph replaced tragedy. All was not lost. Everything became possible again. Pessimism was replaced with optimism. Despair gave way to confidence. Hopes were revived. Among them, inevitably, was the national longing for political independence, with this 'Son of David', victorious over those who had tried to destroy him, even over death itself, back on the throne of David in David's capital of Jerusalem and reigning over David's people for ever, as God had promised.

But it did not happen. After spending two months with his disciples, teaching them about 'the kingdom of God' (Acts 1:3), Jesus revealed his intention to leave earth and return home to his Father in heaven, as if his work was finished and all that he had come to do was done. This took his closest followers, who were all Jewish, by complete surprise, which explains their very last question to him before he left: 'Lord, are you at this time going to restore the kingdom to Israel?' (Acts 1:6, NIV).

Jesus' answer is absolutely crucial. Radically different interpretations have led to both Zionist and anti-Zionist positions. We must spend some time studying this final conversation before his ascension, and do so with great care. So much hangs on our understanding. There are two very different opinions, strongly opposed to one another, representing a deep division among Bible-believing Christians, and profoundly affecting their hopes for the future.

On one side are those who believe the question was itself wrong, betraying ignorance and prejudice, as well as abysmal misunderstanding of Jesus' patient teaching over the previous weeks. And the answer was deliberately evasive and obtuse, with an implicit rebuke for such an inappropriate and even foolish enquiry. Jesus had no intention whatever of becoming an earthly king ruling over the state of Israel. He had come to bring a spiritual kingdom which was 'not of this world'. It would not be established or defended by physical force and was 'from another place' (John 18:36). In spite of his teaching and example, the disciples of Jesus were still thinking in worldly terms, as when Peter attempted to defend his master with a sword in the garden of Gethsemane. The general population were looking for a conqueror who would deliver them from centuries of military occupation (Syrian, Egyptian, Greek and now Roman, ever since the return from exile in Babylon), restoring their political autonomy with their own monarchy and territory. Jesus showed no interest in such expectations. He must have been disappointed, if not dismayed, that his disciples, after three years' training, were still hankering after such thoughts.

Jesus answered: 'It is not for you to know the times or dates the Father has set by his own authority. But you will receive power when the Holy Spirit comes on you; and you will be my witnesses in Jerusalem, and in all Judea and Samaria, and to the ends of the earth' (Acts 1:7–8, NIV). The words suggest a tone of impatience and a rebuke. He is redirecting their attention to the real business of the 'kingdom', to spread the truth about Jesus to the whole world, beginning where they were. Evangelism was the programme, not nationalism.

Such is the argument of one group. I trust I have stated it fairly and accurately, though that is more difficult when you do not agree with it. I believe this interpretation is a distortion of both sides of the conversation and ask the reader to consider an alternative approach.

Every teacher knows that any question is based on assumptions. If these are proper, a straight answer can be given immediately; if any are false, they must be corrected before answering the question. The classic example is: 'Have you stopped beating your wife?' A straight 'Yes' or 'No' has already accepted the presupposition behind the question — that the wife has been beaten, in the past if not the present. Jesus was the greatest teacher there has ever been and he frequently challenged the presumption behind a question, often by asking a question in return (Matthew 19:17 is a typical example).

Behind the disciples' question lay a number of major assumptions, which may be listed as follows:

1. Israel used to have a kingdom.
2. Israel has lost the kingdom.
3. Israel has been promised it will be restored.
4. Jesus can restore it.
5. Jesus will restore it.

They were quite sure about all these, taking them for granted. Their only uncertainty was about the timing, hence their question, a simple 'When?' 'At this time?'

It is striking that Jesus challenged none of their assumptions, much less corrected them. No returned question — 'Where did you get that idea?' No rebuke — 'That's a foolish question.' No hint of impatience — 'How long have I been with you and you still don't understand.' Just a simple answer to a simple question — 'Father has already decided (set) the date for that but it's neither helpful nor necessary for you to know when it is; there's another task that needs to be done before that happens.' In other words, Jesus accepted the question and all the assumptions behind it as perfectly valid and answered accordingly, though he did not satisfy their curiosity.

There may be more to their question than we have seen so far. Why say: 'at this time'? A simple 'when?' would have sufficed, as on other occasions where they had queried timing. Why the emphasis on 'this' and not just 'now'? The context may indicate this unusual phrase. The disciples now recalled and believed so much that he had taught them. They knew he had come from heaven and would soon go back there. They also knew he had promised to make a second visit to earth to complete what he had begun to do on his first. Could 'this time' suggest that they were asking whether the restoration of the kingdom to Israel would take place on this, his first, advent, or would wait until his second? That is, 'this time' or next time? My interpretation of Jesus' answer does not depend on this suggestion nor can I be dogmatic about it, but I present it as a real possibility.

Let me present my interpretations of the whole incident by putting it in the form of a simple parable or parallel:

At the beginning of the Christmas holidays, two boys asked their mother: 'When is Dad going to take us to see a pantomime, before or after Christmas Day? He promised!' The mother replied: 'He's put a date in his diary, but he's keeping it a secret, so you'll have to wait and see. Meanwhile, he wants you to help me to give out some presents to poor children who otherwise won't get any.' Later the two boys discussed what Mum had said. One was quite sure she had avoided a straight answer because: 'She's trying to put us off because Dad has changed his mind. He is not going to take us to a pantomime at all. Knowing him, I'll bet he'll drag us off to that old museum he's always talking about.' The other said: 'I trust my Dad. He never breaks his promises. He must have a good reason for not telling us when. I'm off to help Mum with those presents.' So which boy was right? Only time would tell but one had faith, 'the substance of things hoped for'. Enough said!

Leaving this passage we move on through the New Testament. At another crucial event, the Council of Jerusalem faced the vital question of whether Gentiles had to convert to Judaism if they wanted to follow Jesus, the Jewish Messiah (Acts 15). One of the factors that settled the dispute was an appeal to scripture, a prophecy of Amos (9:11–12). The primary reason why the chairman, the apostle James, used this quotation was its prediction that many Gentiles were part of God's plan, and would bear his name. But it began with a promise to 'rebuild David's fallen tent' (not a reference to his tabernacle worship but his dynasty, just as we talk about the 'house of Windsor'). This passed without comment or correction, indicating it was a belief still held by all present. In passing, we note that the promised restoration of the Davidic dynasty followed the words 'I will return'.

The last book of the Bible, Revelation, which unveils (the meaning of 'apocalyptic') future events, continues the theme of the Davidic dynasty. Christ in glory 'holds the key of David' (3:7). He is 'the Lion of the tribe of Judah, the Root of David' (5:5). He is still 'the Root and the Offspring of David' (22:16).

This chapter is already too long, so let us summarise our conclusions. The new covenant does supersede one of the former covenants made with Israel — the Mosaic, which is designated 'old' and is now obsolete. The other two, the Abrahamic and the Davidic, continue alongside the 'new'. So the 'new' does not rule out the national hopes of the people of Israel (we shall pick this up in Chapter 3), nor even their territorial links (see Chapter 4). These apparently discrepant expectations will be harmonised in the future, with Christ's second advent (Chapter 5).

3

TWO PEOPLES

We ended the first chapter by agreeing with much of what Stephen Sizer is saying, particularly his analysis of the weaknesses and inconsistencies of dispensational Zionism. We begin this third chapter by agreeing with him even more.

He rightly emphasises the new covenant, which is at the heart of the New Testament. Like many evangelicals, he focuses on the crucifixion as its foundation and indeed it was a covenant sealed in blood, as with previous ones. But without the resurrection and ascension, the Old Testament prophecies about it could not have been fulfilled. For example, Ezekiel's promise of the indwelling Spirit could not happen until Jesus was back in heaven and in a position to receive and pour out this divine gift (Acts 2:33).

He rightly points out that the new covenant has established a new people of God, a new humanity. This 'one new man' would be 'made out of two' (Ephesians 2:15), referring to Jew and Gentile, breaking down all barriers between them, both physical in the earthly temple and spiritual in the heavenly. In the latter dimension distinctions of race, gender and class were now irrelevant (Galatians 3:28).

This new people, constituted by faith in Christ, has superseded his 'old' people, who were constituted by flesh from Jacob, grandson of Abraham and later re-named 'Israel' (= he struggles with God). It is difficult to avoid the word 'replacement' for this change, in spite of the facts that the link between them is Jesus the Jewish Messiah and many Jews were the nucleus of the new people. However, this continuity between the two was quickly overshadowed by the discontinuity highlighted by the rapidly growing influx of Gentiles, soon to be the majority component. Inevitably, this new people, the church of Christ, has been largely thought of in Gentile rather than Jewish terms. Over the centuries it has pulled up its Jewish roots, its festivals no longer geared to the Jewish calendar, and even forgotten them altogether.

Sizer and others like him are eager to point out that the New Testament frequently applies Old Testament descriptions of Israel to the church. The clearest example is: 'you (Gentiles) also, like living stones, are being built into a spiritual house, to be a holy priesthood . . .' (1 Peter 2:5, echoing Exodus 19:6). Words like 'chosen' and 'elect' are transferred from one people to the other. This is another arrow in the quiver of the 'supersessionist' case.

He is right to remind his readers that the 'gospel' of the new covenant and its new people is, or ought to be, the primary concern of every Christian. Their priority is the evangelisation of the unbeliever, the edification of the believer, both for the glory of God. To focus any attention on Israel is to him a backward step, a reversion to the old covenant, and identification with the wrong biblical people. His criticism therefore covers all Zionists, since any interest in physical Israel is, for him, a dangerous distraction from priority tasks.

He is rightly concerned about what I would call 'obsessional' Zionists (others have less politely called them 'Israel nutcases'!) I can assure him that those who stand for a balanced biblical Zionism are also embarrassed by, even ashamed of, their excessive preoccupation. Pastors and clergy have frequently told me they would lend a more sympathetic ear to the Zionist case and cause, were it not for one or two 'fanatics' in their congregations (often, I have to add, of the female gender and sometimes, dare I say it, with stronger personalities than their husbands). They quickly find themselves marginalised. They attend prayer meetings for Israel, rather then other intercessory groups, travel miles to hear speakers about Israel, and are openly critical of those who do not share and propagate their convictions, implying that for God, as well as themselves, the attitude to Israel will be the decisive factor in judgement (frequently based on a questionable interpretation of 'brethren' in Matthew 25:40).

However, such extremism, freely admitted, does not of itself bring the Zionist case itself into disrepute, any more than bizarre behaviour negates the biblical realities the charismatic renewal sought to recover. It is a biblical principle to 'let God be true and every man a liar' (Romans 3:4), which means that any views should be tested by his word, not judged by the behaviour of its adherents, though their sincerity can be questioned if inconsistent with their profession.

So back to the Bible to test Sizer's position. I believe we shall find, as in so many cases, that he is right in what he affirms but wrong in what he denies, sound in many of his positive statements, but unsound in his negative inferences. His scriptural data is accurate, but the conclusions he draws not necessarily so.

Take, for example, his valid claim that Old Testament descriptions of Israel are used of the church in the New. That is obviously true and beyond dispute. But how is that to be understood? There are at least two ways of interpreting its significance.

On the one hand, it can be seen as a transfer of function from one people to another, from Israel to the church, which seems to be the way anti-Zionists take it. It is a fundamental assumption of 'replacement' or 'supersessionist' theology. But the logic is flawed. It is a considerable leap from the transfer of some functional language, and a limited amount at that, to believe that everything said to and about Israel in the Old Testament has also been transferred, and an even bigger one to believe it has all been taken away from Israel. It is a slender argument.

On the other hand, it can be understood in an inclusive rather than an exclusive way, meaning that the church now shares in the function that is still God's purpose for Israel, namely to be a light to the world (Isaiah 42:6; 49:6; Matthew 5:14; Luke 2:32; Acts 13:47; 26:23). This application is much more aligned to statements in the New Testament that Christians are now 'fellow citizens *with* God's people' [i.e. Israel] (Ephesians 2:19, not 'instead of' or 'part of' but 'with'); that Gentile Christians have been grafted into the one olive tree of God, alongside Jewish branches (Romans 11:17–18); that Israel's 'calling' is 'irrevocable' (Romans 11:29) and she will one day fulfil it (Romans 11:12, 15).

So the transfer of functional language taken in the context of the whole New Testament, far from demolishing the Zionist case actually builds on it!

Supersessionists are prone to calling Christians 'true Jews' and the church 'new Israel'. Does the New Testament support this usage?

First, the title 'Jew'. Judah (meaning 'praise') was the last tribe to be taken into exile in Babylon and the one who, with the smaller tribe of Benjamin, made up the southern part of the nation after the civil war with and division from the ten tribes in the north, later conquered by Assyria. Since it was the larger of the two tribes, it gave its name to both, which became known as the 'house of Judah'. From its return from Babylon, its citizens became known as 'Jews', which became the name for all survivors of the descendants of Jacob, whatever their original tribe. By the time of Jesus it may have become more commonly used of those who lived in the south of the country around Jerusalem, the original territory of the tribe of Judah and the location of such power as Jews had in the Roman occupation, as opposed to the northerners in Galilee with their own dialect. Some scholars claim that when John's Gospel puts the blame for the execution of Jesus on 'the Jews', only the southerners are given that responsibility. But in the rest of the New Testament 'Jew' is used generally as an ethnic label for any descendant of Jacob.

But there are some passages, notably in Paul, which at first sight suggest a more flexible use of the term, extending it to Gentiles who have faith in the Jewish Messiah. Two statements in his letter have been put together to illustrate this:

'A man is not a Jew if he is only one outwardly . . . . No, a man is a Jew if he is one inwardly, and circumcision is circumcision of the heart . . . . Such a man's praise [meaning of 'Judah'] is not from men, but from God' (Romans 2:28–29).

'Therefore the promise comes by faith, so that it may be by grace and may be guaranteed to all Abraham's offspring — not only those who are of the law [i.e. Jews, under the Mosaic covenant] but also to those [Gentiles] who are of the faith of Abraham. He is the father of us all' (Romans 4:16).

From this conjunction of texts it has been argued that a 'true [i.e. real] Jew' may be used of anyone who shares Abraham's faith, whether Jewish or Gentile in origin. The description is therefore appropriate for any and every Christian.

However, a more careful examination of these and other relevant Pauline texts reveals that he always used 'Jew' and 'Jews' in an ethnic sense and never applied these to Gentile believers (the same goes for all other New Testament writers). He is not saying that all who share Abraham's faith are therefore 'Jews'. He is saying that it is not enough to share Abraham's flesh and be circumcised in body. A genuine Jew in God's sight must *also* share his faith and be circumcised in heart (a state already defined in the Old Testament, Deuteronomy 30:6).

The same goes for the use of the term 'Israel' in the New Testament. Used over seventy times, it invariably has an ethnic meaning, referring to the physical descendants of Abraham through Jacob. The synonym 'Israelite' also occurs (e.g. Romans 11:1; 2 Corinthians 11:22). However, in spite of this general evidence two exceptions are claimed, which open the door to a spiritual meaning of 'Israel', which may therefore be applied to Gentile believers and the church as a whole.

The first is Romans 9:6, 'Not all who are descended from Israel [i.e. Jacob] are Israel [i.e. true, real Israel]'. At first sight, it does look as if the second 'Israel' is not physical but spiritual and therefore can include Gentile believers in the church. Again, a closer examination reveals that Paul is using it as *both* ethnic and spiritual, as with 'Jew' in Romans 2:28. He is referring to the faithful remnant within ethnic Israel, not anyone outside that, the same spiritual core he will later describe (in Romans 11:5).

The second is less clear, namely Galatians 6:16, the one and only text that could be claimed to apply the name 'Israel' to the church. It reads: 'Peace and mercy to all who follow this rule, even to the Israel of God' (New International Version; some other translators insert an extra word without warrant in the Greek text: 'the true Israel of God' e.g. Williams and Phillips). Exegesis raises two questions.

First, what is this 'rule' which is being 'followed' in the first part of the verse? The answer is surely found in the previous verse (15), namely that it does not finally matter whether one is circumcised or uncircumcised, Jew or Gentile. In the earlier context he is battling with those to whom circumcision mattered enormously, indeed was essential to salvation. They had followed him around, trying to persuade his converts that in order to follow a Jewish Messiah they must become Jews and live by the Torah of Judaism. Paul and Peter had both defended the liberty of Gentile believers from all this, at the Council of Jerusalem (Acts 15) but the battle was far from over. What mattered now, since Christ had established the new covenant, was whether anyone had experienced 'the new creation' it had made possible, the radical transformation otherwise known as being 'born again' (John 3:5; 2 Corinthians 5:17).

Second, how do the two parts of the greeting fit together? That is, are 'all' who follow this rule the same group as 'the Israel of God'? The answer very much depends on the translation of the word that links the two phrases. It is the Greek word *kai*, which is generally translated simply 'and', but very occasionally 'even'. 'Even' makes the two phrases synonymous for the same group and would justify calling the 'church' in Galatia and throughout the Gentile world 'the Israel of God', even though this usage would be quite uncharacteristic of Paul. It could be said, and has been, that he has been driven to use this unique exception as a final dig at his Judaising opponents, even though they are Jewish believers in Jesus.

'And' would mean that the two parts of the verse refer to two quite different groups of people: those to whom circumcision is a matter of indifference and those to whom it is a matter of importance. Jewish believers in Jesus clearly come into the latter category. Paul was adamant in his opposition to their insistence on this requirement for his Gentile converts but never once did he insinuate, much less insist, that Jewish believers should cease this practice among themselves. Indeed, he accepted its continuation among them (1 Corinthians 7:18), even circumcising Timothy so that he could evangelise the Jews (Acts 16:3).

In addition to the doubtful translation of *kai* as 'even', there are other considerations favouring this approach. The verse is clearly a greeting: 'Peace and mercy to . . . .' It is not therefore part of the 'didactic' (teaching) section of the letter, an unlikely context in which to make such a radical point. Since in every one of over seventy other references to 'Israel' Paul is using the name in an ethnic sense, it is highly unlikely he would break his habit here. So we may ask why he would use it in this setting.

We need to remember that, while his churches were mainly Gentile in membership, there would usually be some Jews as well. And even his Judaising opponents were also believers in Jesus, even if their proselytising zeal was mistaken. So we can take 'and the Israel of God' as an acknowledgement of these two categories, to whom circumcision did matter; and therefore appropriate recipients of his apostolic blessing. They are the faithful, full of faith, minority of Israel, referred to in Romans 9:6 and 11:5. This interpretation seems to make good sense of the verse. Paul is making sure that the Gentile believers in Galatia do not write off the Jewish ones.

Those who persist in using this verse to attempt to prove that the church has superseded Israel and is entitled to take over her name need to be reminded that it is not considered sound exegesis to base such a far-reaching conclusion on just one verse with debatable translation. That tactic would be dismissed in any other disputed doctrine, as it should in this.

Israel and the church, Jews and Christians, do exist side by side in the world today, as clearly differentiated entities. And there are nations in which Christianity is the 'established' religion as there is now a nation in which Judaism is, though neither is exclusively monofaith, as in some Muslim countries. No-one can deny the existence of Israel, either as a national state or a dispersed people. The question we are discussing is not the existence of Israel, which is self-evident, but whether Israel has been supplanted by the church as God's chosen people on earth, virtually reducing Israel to the status of a Gentile nation, with no special privileges or responsibilities in God's sight. This is the downside of 'supersessionist' theology, a downgrading of God's ancient people.

We have looked at some of the New Testament references most frequently quoted to support this position — and found them less conclusive than many assume. 'Israel' persists as an ethnic entity throughout, acknowledged by the apostles as well as Jesus himself (Matthew 10:6; John 4:22; Romans 1:16).

However, the real question is not the continued existence of Israel, but whether the significance of Israel has also continued. Are they still God's chosen people? Are they still part of God's purpose for the world? Do they have a divine future?

Sizer and his like have laid down the axiom that God cannot possibly have two peoples on earth at the same time. One is tempted to respond to this categorical claim by asking a simple question — why not? Reasons are not clearly given. It is assumed to be a self-evident proposition, like: two plus two = four. Is it a corollary of monotheism, that one God can only have one people at once? It is certainly not a mathematical problem; a three-in-one God would be able to juggle two or more peoples without any difficulty!

Of course, once this statement is accepted, it inevitably follows that the church has superseded Israel as God's people on earth and that settles the whole debate. But is it true to scripture? Is it true at all? Before we look at scripture itself, it may be helpful to ask why the proponents of 'one people at a time' are so adamant.

I believe it is because they are jealous to preserve the New Testament truths of salvation, which is found in Christ alone, as the way, the truth and the life. With this motivation I can only wholeheartedly agree. They fear that acknowledging Israel as still God's people in some way compromises the fact that salvation is exclusively found in Christ, introducing an element of flesh into what is a matter of faith alone.

Such a fear is not entirely groundless. Some Zionists, with more enthusiasm than understanding have slipped into the error called 'dual covenant' the idea that Jews are saved by their own 'old' covenant and Christians are saved by the 'new', through Moses and Jesus respectively. One leading Zionist in America, John Hagee, recently wrote that Jesus did not come to be the Messiah of the Jews, but for the Gentiles (see his book *In Defence of Israel*, excellent material except for chapter 10, to which many have taken exception on the internet). So there is a real danger of distorting the truth of salvation in this way and Zionists need to be aware of it.

But anti-Zionists need to be aware of another danger, that of Israel's 'calling'. What was Israel chosen for? It must be stated emphatically that they were chosen for service, not salvation. They would be the channel through which salvation would be made available to a lost world. And this was fulfilled, through their prophets, priests and kings first, then through the Prophet/Priest/King Jesus, the Jewish Messiah and his Jewish apostles, to say nothing of the Jewish scriptures, the major part of our Bible. Truly, 'salvation is from the Jews' (John 4:22).

But all this never meant that an Israelite or later a Jew was 'saved' because he was a descendant of Jacob. From Abraham onwards they were 'justified' by faith, just as he was (Genesis 15:6). In that respect Israel was on the same basis as any other nation. Only those who believed and went on believing were accepted by God. Those who never believed or fell back into unbelief were rejected (Romans 11:20). Of course, their faith was in the words and promises already spoken to them, long before they knew that Jesus was the Word (John 1:1) and that all the promises would be 'Yes' in him (2 Corinthians 1:20). But it was saving faith. And God can use unbelieving, and therefore unsaved, nations to demonstrate his power and fulfil his purposes.

We have just quoted a verse from Romans 11. That whole chapter, by itself, is enough to refute the notion that Israel is no longer the chosen nation of God, their special relationship to him unchanged, even by their rejection of his Son, their Messiah. God has not rejected them; they are still 'his people' (11:1). They were 'his' in the past, are 'his' in the present and will be 'his' in the future!

Even anti-Zionists acknowledge that some Jews are his, that, 'at the present time there is a remnant chosen by grace' (11:5), as true today as in Paul's day. Paul himself was part and proof of that faithful minority. Now, of course, their faith is in Jesus, the Son, as well as the Father, and they are regarded as part of the church.

But what about 'the others' (11:7), the majority then and now, who are not believers? Have they not missed their opportunity and forfeited their right to be God's special people? The rest of this chapter is all about 'them', even though it is addressed to 'you' Gentile believers. They are still being dealt with by God, though in a negative rather than a positive relationship, their hearts judicially 'hardened', as Pharaoh's had been (9:17–18). In both cases the hardening had been on the human side; the divine side had followed, confirming and reinforcing the voluntary choice involuntarily. Jews are among the hardest people to save, but this did not discourage Paul from trying (11:14; cf. 9:3 and 10:1) and should not dishearten us either (though it must be admitted that some Zionists do not share Paul's yearning or make evangelism a priority).

The hardening is neither total nor permanent. The situation is not beyond redemption. They are still 'his people' and God has not given up on them. They were 'broken off' but can be grafted back in again and will take place in their own olive tree more readily than the 'wild' Gentiles that have taken their place. This is the only 'replacement' teaching in Paul. Some, not all, of the Jewish branches, not the roots or trunk of the Jewish tree, have been replaced by Gentiles. And this could easily be reversed. Gentile believers could be cut off as Jews, if they do not continue in divine grace (verses 20–22 are the death-knell to the cliché: 'once saved, always saved'). Jewish unbelievers can be restored if they come back to faith.

Astonishingly, Paul not only affirms they can be but seems to assume that they will be, anticipating such a blessing for the whole world as they resume their calling (11:12 and 15). No less than the gifts God gave to ethnic Israel, chief of which was their own land. The calling still belongs to them as well (11:29), and God has future plans for the faithless rump of Israel just as much as the faithful remnant. Both parts are still 'his people'. To deny this is to be guilty of arrogant contempt (11:18, 20, 25), the very opposite of an appropriate attitude of faith in and fear of the Lord (11:20).

All this is building up to a statement, the importance of which cannot be exaggerated in this whole debate, namely 11:25–27. So crucial is the interpretation of it that we must take great care and much time to unpack it.

Paul calls it a 'mystery'. Two mistakes in unpacking this word are common. One is taken from English usage and is akin to 'mysterious', something beyond human comprehension, inexplicable, contrary to reason, to be blindly accepted. None of this is in Paul's mind, in spite of many sermons and preachers! For him, a 'mystery' is a secret that can now be made public; a divine intention which human reason could not have discovered, but which has now been revealed and may be repeated.

The other mistake is to assume that whenever Paul uses the word 'mystery' he is referring to the same revealed secret, particularly the one that incorporates Gentiles in his purposes (Ephesians 3:6). But here in Romans it is not about Gentiles but about Israel. And the essence of it is that some day in the future 'all Israel will be saved' (11:26). Each word is important so we must take it step by step.

'Saved' always means for Paul salvation from sin's penalty, power and pollution; justification, sanctification and glorification, by grace and through faith, all exclusively in the Lord Jesus Christ. This is what it means in this whole letter to the Romans and in this particular section of it about the Jewish people (see 10:1 and 11:14). It is the salvation which some Jews and many Gentiles have already found by calling on the name of the Lord, believing in their hearts and confirming with their mouths (10:9–13). The verb is in the future tense so this had not yet happened when Paul wrote. Nor indeed has it yet happened in our day. While an increasing number of Jews are coming to Christ for salvation, it is still only a small minority, by no stretch of the imagination could it be called 'all Israel'.

'All' — what does this mean? It cannot mean all Jews who have ever lived. Had it done so, Paul would not have suffered such pain over their state (9:1–3), nor prayed so much for their salvation (10:1), nor made such an effort to win them (11:14). He clearly believed many of his 'brothers of his own race' were facing a lost eternity. He was even willing to be banished from Christ if it would get them to heaven. Zionists need to be constantly reminded of this. They can be so caught up in 'comforting' Israel that they forget that converting them is the greatest service they can render. Preparing them for the next world is far more important than providing for them in this. (Zionists are not the only Christians for whom philanthropy takes priority over evangelism in 'mission'.)

Nor does it necessarily mean all Jews still living when it happens. It may indicate this, but a precedent for the phrase 'all Israel' exists in the Old Testament, forty-eight times, to be exact. Sometimes it is a reference to the general spiritual and moral state of the nation. At other times it refers to a large assembly representing every part of the nation, all twelve tribes or all elders. In neither case does it mean every single Israelite, every man, woman and child. We may therefore translate the New Testament phrase as 'Israel as a whole' or 'Israel *en masse*'. We may add that Israel is the only nation on earth that can claim a biblical promise of a national revival (even though many Christians today try to claim 2 Chronicles 7:14 as a promise for 'their land').

'Israel' has been taken so far in its ethnic sense, referring to physical Israel and especially its unbelieving majority, which has been in view since verse 7. And 'Israel' means exactly this at the very beginning of the statement we are examining: 'Israel has experienced a hardening . . .' (11:25). It would be strange indeed if a word was to change so radically in meaning within the confines of a single sentence, to say nothing of the fact that every other time 'Israel' is used throughout this section of

Paul's letter (chapter 9–11) it is always used in an ethnic way.

Yet Sizer, quoting Calvin, who appealed to Galatians 6:16 (see above), claims that 'Israel' in Romans 11:26 is used in a spiritual sense and refers to the completed church, including all its Jewish and Gentile members, not an end-time revival of ethnic Israel 'as a whole'. Is there any ground for this interpretation in the text itself? Yes, they say. It lies in one key word we have not yet discussed.

'*So* all Israel will be saved.' Zionists are prone to think and even quote as if the word is 'then'. That is, after the full number of Gentiles is in, then all Israel will be saved. But their critics are right to point out that the word is 'thus' rather than 'then'. The Greek word *houtos* certainly means 'thus' or 'in this way' or 'just so' or 'as a result', and relates to a previous statement as the cause of the result (it is also the word translated 'so' in John 3:16; it does not mean 'so much' but 'in the same way', referring back to verses 14 and 15, and 'so' should really come before 'God').

So what is the cause that has resulted in 'all Israel' being saved? Those who rule out a national revival of ethnic Israel point to the preceding clause, arguing that the fullness of the Gentiles (nations), together with any converted Jews has completed the church, the spiritual Israel. Israel as a whole, all Israel. But the clause about the Gentile fullness is a subsidiary clause of the whole sentence, qualifying the main clause, which states that the judicial hardening of ethnic Israel is both partial and temporary, to be removed when all Gentiles are in. It is the removal of this hardening by the God who imposed it, that will cause the ready acceptance of salvation by Israel 'as a whole', who are so much more easily grafted into their own olive tree as 'natural' branches. 'So' makes entire sense in this way.

It is difficult to avoid the conclusion that God can and does have two peoples on earth at the present time — his church, made up of some Jews and more Gentiles, all of whom believe in Jesus, and his people 'Israel', still in an unbelieving state. The former are the fruit of the gospel, having received the mercy of God. The latter are foes of the gospel, yet to receive his mercy. Their spiritual salvation is intertwined, each affecting the other, both negatively and positively (11:30–31). Both are loved by God.

But their separate identity is temporary. It is the divine plan 'to bring all things in heaven and on earth together under one head, even Christ' (Ephesians 1:10, and 'even' is not *kai*, but *en* = in). This consummation includes Israel and the church, together having found salvation in him. Surely this is what Jesus meant when he said: 'I have other sheep which are not of this fold. [Gentiles outside Israel.] I must bring them also. They too will listen to my voice, and there shall be one flock and one shepherd' (John 10:16). Then, and only then, will it be possible to use 'church' and 'Israel' as interchangeable synonyms. Until then we should keep them separate and distinct.

To summarise this chapter, Sizer is absolutely right to emphasise the new covenant and the radical changes it has introduced to the narrative of our redemption.

It has created a new community, at the same time broader than Israel, in being truly international, and narrower, in depending on individual faith. It is neutral towards gender, race or class, and indifferent to heredity. God has no grandsons now.

It has created a new cultus, rendering obsolete the temple, its priesthood and sacrifices. Worship is based on the local synagogue rather than the central temple, with its chairs and orchestras. God looks for worship in spirit and truth (reality).

It is the inferences Sizer and others imply which raise the real problems for Zionists. Among them are:

i. That everything in the Old Testament belongs to the 'old' covenant and is transformed or annulled by the 'new'. We dealt with that in chapter 2.

ii. That God can only have one covenant people at any one time. This chapter has examined that.

iii. That the land of Israel is now irrelevant to God's plan and purpose. See chapter 4.

iv. That all the promises to Israel have already found fulfilment in Jesus. See chapter 5.

4

THE PROMISED LAND

If the Jews are still 'his people', then the land must still be theirs. If ethnic Israel is still special, then territorial Israel is as well.

This logic may be obvious to some but to others it is by no means clear. Indeed, those who think this way are often charged with having an Old Testament mindset, where it is freely admitted that people and place are inextricably bound together. Yet one statement in the New Testament would, by itself, corroborate both parts of the proposition: they (ethnic Israelites) are loved on account of the patriarchs (i.e. Abraham, Isaac and Jacob) for, 'God's gifts and his call are irrevocable' (Romans 11:28b–29). When the covenant with the patriarchs is carefully examined (in Genesis 12–17), by far the most prominent 'gift' is the 'land', never to be taken away.

This is the heart of the difference between Zionists and their critics. The former believe that God has brought his people back to their own land, according to his promises, and that therefore they have a divine right to be there. The latter regard their return as a political event with no biblical or theological significance. This fault-line runs right through the Christian church, creating a gulf that cannot be bridged until one side or the other see the 'error' of their ways.

The question is put quite simply in the title of a book by a Jewish believer, Dr Arthur Kac: *The Rebirth of the State of Israel — is it of God or of Men?* This was one of the first books I read on the subject and one of the factors which led to my own convictions. I can highly recommend it but I think it is now out of print (it was published in 1958 by Marshall, Morgan and Scott).

So was it a purely political event or a providential one? Can it be fully explained in natural terms or does it require supernatural factors? Was it the result of human ambition and endeavour or was it a divine intervention? Of course, a 'miracle' can be viewed from both angles, an event combining human and divine activity (witness the crossing of the Red Sea in Exodus 14).

There certainly is a human side to the story of 'Israel', the people and the place. It goes back to the foundation of the nation. Liberated from slavery in Egypt, they began the trek to the land promised to their fathers. They had been kept out of it until the inhabitants had forfeited every moral right to live there or even anywhere (Genesis 15:16). They entered, conquered and settled most of it.

Now they would learn the hard way that their ownership of the land was unconditional, under the Abrahamic covenant, but the occupation of the land was conditional, under the Mosaic covenant.

Their calling was to be a visible demonstration to other nations of divine blessing on those who lived the right way and curse on those who lived the wrong way. The punishments for the latter would range from difficulties to dangers, from drought and pestilence, through invasion and occupation, to the ultimate deportation and exile.

The first exile to Babylon lasted seventy years, because the seventh year of fallow rest for the land had been neglected for nearly five centuries. In passing we note that not all Israelites were taken away from the land (the minority who stayed married local Gentiles, producing the mixed breed Samaritans). Nor did all those taken return. In fact only some thousands came back to rebuild the nation (the 'wise men' who came to Bethlehem at Jesus' birth could have been descendants of those who stayed).

The pre-exilic prophets (from Joel to Isaiah) had given ample warning and adequate reasons for the disaster. But they had also conveyed divine assurances of a return after the disciplinary action. One of the exiles, Daniel, claimed this in prayer to God. Another, Nehemiah, petitioned a Gentile king. God made it possible through an alien ruler, Cyrus of Persia. Note the combination of human and divine activity in this return from the first exile, four centuries before Christ.

There was to be a second exile from the land, more severe than the first. It would last much longer (nineteen centuries), scatter the nation far more widely to the four 'corners' of the earth: north, east, south and west, and lead to far worse suffering (culminating in the Holocaust, *Shoah* in Hebrew).

Since God always gave fair warning and clear explanation of his judgements, one is bound to ask what sin led to this tragedy and who predicted it. The answer to both questions is to be found in Jesus. He both foresaw and foretold it and pointed to Israel's rejection of himself, their failure to recognise in his ministry a day of divine visitation (Luke 19:44). They had 'disowned the holy and Righteous One . . . killed the author of life' (Acts 3:13, 15). They had refused to listen to the prophet like Moses (Deuteronomy 18:15; cf. Matthew 21:11; Acts 3:22–23).

The second exile began with the siege and destruction of Jerusalem by the Romans in AD 70, reaching a climax in AD 135 with a final revolt under a false messiah, Bar Kochba, and the mass suicide on Masada. Jews were banished from their capital and its environs, rebuilt with a Gentile name (Aelia

Capitolina),while their country was renamed Palestinia (after the Philistines, as a final insult).

However, in spite of popular myth, not all Jews were removed from the land. As with the exile, some remained, though they survived in communities remote from Jerusalem, as in Safed in Upper Galilee (almost certainly the place Jesus called 'a city set on a hill').

Nor was the land removed from the Jews. Wherever they went they carried their homeland in their hearts. At their annual remembrance of the founding of their nation (at the Feast of Passover), their mutual greeting was: 'Next year in Jerusalem'. They had undying longing to go back home.

And some of them did. Throughout the ages a trickle of Jews made '*aliya*' (the Hebrew word for 'go up') to the temple in Jerusalem — the last word in the Jewish scriptures (in our Bibles: 2 Chronicles 36:23). They often lived in extreme deprivation, surviving on financial support from the Diaspora (dispersed Jews in other countries).

The return began in earnest in the last quarter of the nineteenth century, partly as a result of pogroms (waves of persecution) in Russia. A small estate was built outside the western wall of Jerusalem. (It is still there, marked by a windmill, and contains the home of the well-known Messianic Jew, Lance Lambert). Tracts of land, often malaria-ridden swamps, were purchased from absentee Arab landlords, drained and planted with thirsty eucalyptus trees from Australia. The desolate landscape described by Mark Twain and painted by David Roberts began to be transformed into productive farmland. It meant, of course, that former professionals, doctors, scientists, bankers, had to learn manual skills. The growing economy attracted thousands of Arab immigrants and gave them employment. Co-operative communities, *kibbutzim* and *moshavim* (the former nearer to 'communist' practice than the latter) sprang up like mushrooms.

Britain was to play a major role, for better and worse. In

establishing a consulate and an Anglican church and bishopric in the old city of Jerusalem (Christ Church, just inside the Jaffa Gate), she was in a position to encourage and support Jewish immigration in spite of the occupation of Palestine by the Moslem Turks of the Ottoman Empire. All this was in the middle of the nineteenth century, before the first major *aliya*.

British troops under General Allenby liberated Jerusalem from the Turks in 1917. After the First World War, the League of Nations gave Britain the Mandate to govern Palestine. Alas, promises were made to both Jews and Arabs in the region that were incompatible. British governments favoured the Jewish cause while the Foreign Office backed the Arab. Inevitably, tension arose between them, erupting in violence.

The infamous White Paper of 1939 severely limited Jewish immigration just when it was most needed for escape from Germany. Even after World War II, Jews leaving Europe were detained in camps in Cyprus. The situation in Palestine became so difficult that Britain pulled out in 1947, leaving the Jews to declare a sovereign State of Israel the next year and the surrounding Arab nations to declare war, with the intention of driving the infant intruder into the (Mediterranean) Sea. Their survival in this and subsequent conflicts is the stuff of legend. Conventional attacks have now given way to missiles and suicide bombers.

Such are the bare bones of the human side of the story of the return of Jews to 'their own land', the land God promised to their forefathers. Is there a divine side to the story? What part, if any, did God himself play? Can it be explained in natural terms as a political event or does it reveal supernatural aspects making it a providential intervention?

These questions strike at the very heart of Christian Zionism, based as it is on the conviction that God has brought the people and the place back together, in accordance with his word and that they therefore have a divine right to be there. But they are valid, even vital, questions. And the onus is on Zionists to answer them. As one of them, I have had to examine my own thinking and found there are three main reasons why I am convinced about divine involvement — God's sovereignty over history, the unfulfilled prophecies of the Bible and circumstantial evidence.

SOVEREIGNTY OVER HISTORY

One of the obvious assumptions of the Old Testament is that God has ultimate control over the destiny of nations as well as individuals. Supremely this was demonstrated in the case of his chosen nation, Israel, bringing them out of Egypt and into Canaan. But to do this he had to show his power over Egypt as well. Not many seem to have noticed that he brought the Philistines from Crete (Amos 9:7), around the same time and to the same place! The Israelites up in the mountains would be threatened by the Philistines on the coastal plain.

The Lord 'drove out the nations before them' when they entered the land under Joshua and stopped doing so when they betrayed his trust (Judges 2:22). He disciplined Israel by bringing surrounding peoples into their territory (Arameans, Midianites, Amalekites, Moabites, Ammonites, etc. (Judges 1–11.) These were quite small kingdoms, Israel's immediate neighbours. But God was no less able to control great powers. He could raise up Assyria, Babylon, and Persia, use them for his own purpose, then bring them down to nothing when they abused the power he gave them.

We could say that the God of Israel is the one who draws and redraws the political atlas of the world. This sovereignty over time and space is both assumed and affirmed in the New Testament. Paul, addressing the intellectual elite in Greece, makes the explicit claim that God decides the portion of history and geography occupied by any and every nation (Acts 17:26).

No-one can deny the simple fact that well over one third of the Jewish people are back in 'their own land'. The name 'Israel' is back on the map after centuries of absence. If God is responsible for the arrival and departure of all peoples, nations and empires, then it must follow that he is responsible for the reappearance on the stage of history of the nation-state of Israel. He has brought them back again for the 'second' time (Isaiah 11:11).

And if divine sovereignty underlies all national movements, how much more must this apply to the nation he chose as his own and with which he has identified himself as 'the Holy One of Israel' (numerous times in Isaiah). This brings us to the second biblical reason for believing their return is of his doing:

UNFULFILLED PROPHECIES

The Jewish prophets were not all 'doom and gloom'. Even Jeremiah, whose name has become a byword for depressing pessimism, frequently used the word 'hope'. Though convinced exile was inevitable, because of national idolatry and immorality, he held out the promise of ultimate return (read chapters 16, 23, 24, 30, 31, 32, 46), as did his predecessor Isaiah (read chapters 43, 52, 60, 61, 62, 65, 66) and his successor Ezekiel (read chapters 34, 36, 37, 39).

To summarise succinctly the consistent message of these 'major' and other 'minor' prophets — the nation had turned away from the Lord and must be turned out of his land, but he would always bring them back to the land and back to himself. Predictions about this physical/spiritual return are so numerous that they cannot be ignored. One scholar has listed over one hundred references. But they can be interpreted and applied in four different ways:

First: the **historical**. This applies all of these promises to the return from the Babylonian exile in the fifth century BC. There is therefore no need to look for any further fulfilment in the future. God kept his word in the distant past and it is unwarranted and misleading to link it with the contemporary present.

At first sight, this approach seems to settle the matter quite simply, but it is too simple. It does not do justice to the Old Testament data, when it is examined in detail.

i. We have already mentioned Isaiah's forecast of a 'second' return (11:11; a text made much of in his autobiographical account of his Zionist views, *The Chariots of Israel*, by the former Labour Prime Minister Harold Wilson).

ii. Then there is the obvious presence of promises of ultimate return in post-exilic prophets, after the return from Babylon (e.g. Zechariah 8:7–8; 14:10–11).

iii. Some predictions clearly anticipate a worldwide return, from the four corners of the earth; from the north, south, east and west; from the islands of the sea (e.g. Isaiah 11:11–12) — whereas the return from Babylon was only from one country and one direction (north-east).

iv. Other predictions foresee a final and permanent return, never to lose the land again (e.g. Jeremiah 24:5–6), which was not the case when they came back from Babylon.

v. Some anticipate a total re-gathering of all the scattered. Only a minority left Babylon — about 45,000.

In all these points we are witnessing a characteristic of Hebrew prophecy. A prediction can be fulfilled more than once, even in a triple as well as a double realisation (cf. Isaiah 7:14 came true in King Ahaz's day and in Mary, Matthew 1:22–23; Daniel 11:31 in Antiochus Epiphanes, 175 BC, yet again after Jesus, Matthew 24:15).

We conclude that the promises of return were only partially fulfilled after the first exile and their full actualisation will take place at the end of the second exile, which is happening in our own time.

Second, the **conditional**. This approach agrees that the prophecies were only partially fulfilled in the return from Babylon, but does not expect any further fulfilment, on the grounds that the promises have been forfeited by the Jewish rejection of their own Messiah, Jesus, the Son of God. Since the people of Israel have not kept their part of their covenant with God, he is released from his obligations and does not need to keep his promises. The second exile is therefore permanent, an expression of divine severance of the nation as such from himself. The land is now irrelevant to his purposes and regaining any of it is purely political, a historical, rather than a theological event, the result of human rather than divine activity.

We have already said all that needs to be said about the inadequacy of this position. Its basic flaw is that it confuses the Mosaic with the Abrahamic covenants, failing to recognise that the former was conditional with 'you must' demands matching the 'I will' offers, whereas the latter was unconditional, full of 'I will' promises, without 'you must' requirements. Exile from the land was a consequence of breaking the Mosaic covenant, the ultimate return to the land a consequence of the unbreakable Abrahamic covenant, so emphatically affirmed in the New Testament (Hebrews 6:13–18).

However, some Bible scholars claim that the promises of return were conditional, depending on proven repentance of the sins that had led them into exile. Certainly there are a number of texts which directly connect a return to the land with a return to the Lord. Earlier Christian Zionists expected the physical and spiritual returns to happen simultaneously. Some even expected the spiritual to precede the physical.

But neither has happened with the current restoration. Israel is a secular state, as irreligious and morally decadent as many Western democracies. Tel Aviv feels little different from San Francisco or Copenhagen. There is a religious undertone to culture and calendar, but no more than in Britain.

This has given anti-Zionists a reason for scepticism about Zionist claims that God is keeping his promises in the current return. The return to the land does not seem to have been accompanied by a return to the Lord. Tourists and pilgrims in Israel have been surprised, even shocked, to find so many godless Jews, often giving themselves all the credit for recovering their ancient territory. Christian Zionists have to face this conundrum as well as others, in fact more so. How have they coped?

First, they have noticed, after careful study of the biblical prophecies, that where a chronological sequence is clearly indicated, the physical return to the land precedes the spiritual return to the Lord. Readers are invited to check the following scriptures — Isaiah 4:2–3; Jeremiah 33:6–9; Ezekiel 36:24–26; 37:1–14; Joel 2:18–29; Zechariah 13:8–9. Is there any evidence that this will happen? Yes, it is already happening!

Second, since the establishment of the State of Israel in 1948 there have been some significant spiritual changes. Attitudes to Jesus of Nazareth have undergone a major shift from negative criticism to positive appreciation. Jewish scholars are writing favourable assessments of his ministry. Still falling short of full Christian understanding of his divinity or even his Messiahship, he is being hailed as a charismatic teacher, even as a prophet. When a leading Rabbi says: 'If when the Messiah comes it turns out to be Jesus of Nazareth, I cannot think of a single Jewish objection', something new is happening, in spite of centuries of anti-Semitism in the Christian church. Hebrew New Testaments are openly studied in schools and colleges. This trend may have further to go, but it is heading in the right direction.

Even more striking is the rapid increase in Jewish believers in Jesus, both inside the State of Israel and outside in the Diaspora (I don't call them 'Jewish Christians' because that is a contradiction in terms, 'Christian' being a nickname coined by and for Gentiles; Acts 11:26). In 1948 the number of Israeli believers could almost be counted on two hands. Now they are counted in thousands, presenting a real headache to the Chief Rabbinate, who seem to think it is the result of Gentile missionary invasion. But it is an indigenous, spontaneous happening. Most Gentile Christians in the world don't even know about it, even those who have been there! At the same time, a parallel movement is happening in the Diaspora. Jews for Jesus! This has made an astonishing impact. Messianic synagogues are springing up in the Western world.

Some would call this 'revival'. It is certainly a return to the very early church situation, where the apostles, elders, deacons and most of the members were Jewish. In those days the issue was whether Gentiles could follow Jesus without becoming Jews (Acts 17). Now it is whether Jews can follow Jesus without becoming Gentiles. For all the issue is how to be 'one new man' in him while not being neutered in culture. But it is a welcome problem, to see a Jewish church re-emerging after all this time.

The test is time. It was the famous preacher Phillips Brooks who said: 'The trouble is that I'm in a hurry and God isn't!' If so many have already found salvation in *Yeshua HaMashiach* since they had their own country again, it does not stretch faith very far to believe that 'all Israel will be saved' (we explored this prediction in chapter 3).

But there are still two more ways of interpreting the promises of return to the land, which we must consider:

Third, the **allegorical**. Granted that the Old Testament predictions are presented in physical terms, a physical return of physical people to a physical land, many believe that, in the light of New Testament principles, they must now be understood in spiritual terms, to be applied to God's spiritual people, the church. The physical kingdom of Israel has been superseded by the spiritual kingdom of God/heaven, which is universal, not territorial, internal rather than external, established by love, not force (texts such as Luke 17:21 and John 18:36 are favourite quotations for this viewpoint). This was the mistake the apostles made in their final question to Jesus before his ascension (Acts 1:7; but we have already argued against this in chapter 2).

This, of course, is how 'replacement' theology *has* to

interpret the Old Testament promises. Ethnic Israel is no longer part of God's plans and purposes, but has been 'replaced' by the church. This 'new' or 'true' Israel has inherited all the blessings promised to the old Israel (but none of the curses!) No-one seems to draw the conclusion that the church has a divine right to that part of the Middle East between the Nile and the Euphrates (though many branches of the Christian church have readily planted a stake in Jerusalem, but not in Tel Aviv where most Israelis live, betraying more interest in the place than the people).

Promises regarding the 'land' are transmuted into 'earth' (as in Matthew 5:5) or 'world' (as in Romans 4:13), universalised as well as spiritualised. I cannot help wondering how Abraham, Isaac and Jacob feel about their misunderstanding of God's oath to them! The poor things thought the real estate was a permanent legacy, not a temporary loan!

A more subtle form of all this is beginning to spread under the label 'fulfilment' theology. Instead of a straight transfer of promises from Israel to the church, an intermediate stage is inserted in the process. The promises were both focused and fulfilled in one person who in himself represented true Israel on his own, namely Jesus. Then through him the promises were extended to his church, made up of Jewish and Gentile —believers in him. Advocates often use the analogy of an hour-glass, the wide Israel narrowing down to one Israelite then broadening out again into the church, the continuity between the two peoples found in only one person. An oft-quoted text to support this idea is: 'For no matter how many promises God has made, they are "Yes" in Christ' (2 Corinthians 1:20, NIV). Advocates protest that this is not 'replacement' thinking, though the practical implications are somewhat similar, even though Jesus is seen as the unique link between Jew and Christian, Israel and the church.

We make the following comments:

i. Does scripture really support the idea that the faithful

remnant of Israel (7000 in Elijah's day) shrank down to just one in Jesus? What about Simeon and Anna, Nathaniel later, and above all Mary, the mother of Jesus? And would Paul have talked about God's chosen remnant by grace 'right up to the present time' (Romans 11:5), if there had been none but Jesus at one time?

ii. The 'hour-glass' figure is hardly consistent with Paul's analogy of the olive tree, in which wild olive branches (Gentile believers) have been grafted in 'among the others' (Romans 11:17, referring to faithful Jewish believers not cut out of their own tree). There is no hint that these were ever reduced to one.

iii. The fatal flaw in this 'fulfilment' thinking is the assumption that all the promises to Israel have already been fulfilled in Christ and must therefore be reinterpreted to fit into what he said and did during his first coming to earth. But there are predictions in both Old and New Testaments that have not yet happened and may be presumed to be postponed until his second visit to our planet. He must reign until all his enemies are under his feet (1 Corinthians 15:25). Jerusalem will be trodden down by Gentiles until . . . (Matthew 23:39). Unbelieving Jews will remain hardened until the fullness of Gentiles are in (Romans 11:25). There are many promises in the New Testament yet to be fulfilled. And in the Old Testament, scholars are agreed that promises about Jesus' first and second comings are intermingled, even integrated, as two mountain peaks seen together through a telescope, yet having a valley between them. What we can say is that all the promises of God have been or will be fulfilled in Christ. To put them all into his first coming inevitably leads to distorted interpretation.

iv. There is a conspicuous absence of any clear explanation of how Jesus fulfilled in himself the promise of a return to the land. He was never in exile from it, unless his being forsaken by his Father during his crucifixion is claimed for this, but this seems a rather forced analogy.

In conclusion, both the 'replacement' and 'fulfilment' theologies are inevitably driven to the allegorical interpretation of God's promises to Israel, and this invariably leads to variations, even disagreements, over meaning and application. Let readers look up the very different senses given to the 'wolf' and the 'lamb' in Isaiah 11:6 as an example. The simplest way is to take it at face value as a prediction of the redemption of nature 'red in tooth and claw' (Tennyson), for which the whole creation groans (Romans 8:22). Which brings us to the final way of interpreting the promises of a return to the land.

Fourth, the **literal**. One of the most common accusations brought against Christian Zionists is that they take the Bible too literally. Curiously, Sizer takes this one step further. After an opening section appealing for a more literal reading of scripture, he goes on to accuse Zionists of being 'ultra-literalist', without really defining what he means — perhaps taking the Bible more literally than he does or more than he thinks they should.

No-one I know takes the whole Bible literally. Passages that clearly indicate that they are meant metaphorically are taken that way. Others that contain symbols are understood accordingly. In the book of Revelation the dragon represents the devil and the scarlet woman a city. But behind every symbol and metaphor lie realities.

The underlying principle behind taking scripture literally unless it is clearly indicated otherwise is the simple confidence that God means what he says and says what he means. He is not trying to be obscure or mysterious. The inspired writings were not intended for scholars or theologians but for ordinary people in everyday language. We may need help today to know what the original writers intended or the original readers understood, with information about background and culture (see my book: *Unlocking the Bible* Omnibus edition; Harper Collins). But for the most part all that is needed is an open mind and the Holy Spirit.

Anyone reading the promises to Israel of a full and final return to their own land will assume that they mean exactly that — unless, that is, they have been told that they cannot mean that! If they are reading through the Bible they will already have read that 'God is not a man, that he should lie, nor a son of man, that he should change his mind. Does he speak and then not act? Does he promise and not fulfil?' (Numbers 23:19; 1 Samuel 15:29).

But there is more to it than a naïve trust in the plain sense of scripture. Few realise how packed with predictions about the future the Bible actually is. Just under a quarter of the verses (24%) contain a promise of what God plans to do. Altogether well over 700 future events are forecast, most just once, some repeatedly and a few many times (the Lord's Second Coming is mentioned over 300 times). Of these, just under 600 have already come true (81%, to be precise). It does not need much faith to believe that the rest will follow.

Those that were future and are now past were fulfilled quite literally. To take just one example, Ezekiel predicted that the city of Tyre would be thrown into the sea. Centuries later Alexander the Great marched on the city, but the inhabitants fled for safety to an island half a mile offshore. Alexander had an army but no navy; but he was not called 'the Great' for nothing. He ordered the deserted city to be razed to the ground and every bit of stone and timber to be used to build a causeway through the sea to the island, so that he could kill or capture its inhabitants. The present city is out on what is now a peninsula, the site of the former city a bare rock where fishermen spread their nets to dry, exactly as the prophet said it would be (Ezekiel 26:4–5). No other city in history, before or since, has ever suffered such a fate. Statisticians have calculated the chances of it happening at one in ten to the power of 39!

To put it another way, if all the prophecies relating to the first advent (born in Bethlehem, brought up in Galilee, etc.)

were literally fulfilled, why should it be thought that those relating to the second advent need to be understood in quite a different way? Why should it be considered so crass to take them all literally? Is there a theological snobbery at work here?

If 'literalism' means interpreting scripture literally where it clearly intends to be taken that way and metaphorically where the text or context clearly indicates it is to be taken that way, then Christian Zionists happily accept that label. If by 'ultra-literalist', Sizer means no recognition that some scriptures are allegorical or metaphorical but all are to be taken literally, most, if not all, Zionists would protest. The only issue is which scriptures are to be taken one way and which another. Too often this is decided by theological presuppositions brought to the text rather than the text itself. It requires more study and greater skill to let the Bible speak for itself.

It is, perhaps, appropriate at this point, before we turn from scripture to other reasons for believing God has brought his people back to their land, to face a common objection raised by anti-Zionists. They ask: 'Why is nothing said about such a return in the New Testament?' It is a valid question but usually carries undertones of scepticism. However, it must be answered.

The first thing is to challenge an assumption hinted at in the question itself, namely that if something is not stated in the New Testament it is of secondary interest and importance to the Christian. It cannot be emphasised too strongly that the 'canon' (rule) of scripture for Christians contains both Old and New Testaments, equally the inspired and authoritative word of God. A statement in the Old does not need to be corroborated in the New to be accepted as true. To suggest otherwise is to fall into the trap of having 'a canon within the canon', that is, using one part of scripture to test the authenticity of another. It is a common error (e.g. using the Jesus of the Gospels to discount the Jesus of Revelation). What we are saying is that the mere fact of non-repetition in the New of clear promises in the Old is not of itself sufficient reason to disregard or even discard them.

Of course, where the New Testament specifically declares Old Testament material to be altered or annulled, as in the case of the Mosaic covenant (see chapter 2), that is decisive. But to assume, without clear statements to that effect, that solemn promises made under oath are either obsolete or changed beyond recognition is surely unwarranted.

There are other reasons why the land is not as prominent in the New Testament as in the Old. One is that most books of the New Testament were written before the second exile commenced (in AD 70) or was consummated (in AD 135), so the question of a return never arose. This applies to the first three Gospels, Matthew, Mark and Luke (often called 'Synoptic' because of their common context and viewpoint, so different from John), Acts and Paul's letters. Two books, obviously addressed to Jewish readers, might have mentioned a return but were written before Jews had left. Matthew was written in the 60s (as proven from a fragment in the library of Magdalen College, Oxford) and Hebrews would hardly have argued against the Jews going back to priesthood and sacrifices if they had already ceased.

The other side to this is that most of the New Testament books were written for largely, if not exclusively, Gentile communities, now partakers with (not 'as') Israel in the blessings of the new covenant. A return to the land was irrelevant to their expectations of the future, their 'hope' in God. However, it is highly significant that in his letter to the Roman church (a mixed community of Jewish and Gentile believers), Paul addresses one section (chapters 9–11) directly to the Gentiles and reminds them of what they owe to the Jews. It is in this context that he states that God still has a special relationship with ethnic Israel, 'his people', even the unbelieving majority whom he has temporarily 'hardened', as well as the faithful remnant, that he has future plans for their salvation. He adds, almost as an aside, that back of all this is his permanent concern for and commitment to their forefathers, 'the patriarchs', Abraham, Isaac and Jacob. His gifts to them are 'irrevocable' (11:29). The one gift mentioned throughout the account of the Abrahamic covenant (Genesis 12:7) is the land as a permanent possession of his descendants. This verse alone is enough New Testament endorsement of the Old Testament promises of a full and final return.

The land does have a major role in the New Testament. It is the stage on which the drama of our redemption was played out, the location of Jesus' birth, life, death, resurrection and ascension. And the church begins there but soon spreads into other countries. All this is accepted and acknowledged. The crucial question is whether the land of Israel figures in any New Testament predictions about the future or whether it is simply left behind as the Gentile world embraces the Christian faith.

Even in the Gospels there are strong hints that the land will have a part in the future, especially in the final events of the present era. Within the so-called 'apocalyptic' (unveiling of things to come) discourse of Jesus, recorded in Matthew 24, Mark 13, and Luke 21, there are specific references to Jerusalem. On other occasions Jesus clearly anticipated a second visit to the city (Matthew 23:39).

There may well be a reference to the unfulfilled prophecies of a national return to the land in Acts 3:21, where Peter, referring to the Lord's Second Coming, says: 'He must remain in heaven until the time comes for God to restore everything, as he promised long ago through his holy prophets.' The onus is on those who believe this excludes all prophetic promises of a full and final reunion of the people and the place to prove the point. Peter's Jewish audience would almost certainly include them as they pondered his words. He himself may have recalled the disciples' final question to Jesus before his ascension and his answer (Acts 1:6–7, discussed in Chapter 2).

The book of Revelation continues these themes. The first

half focuses on the people of Israel and their survival during the perilous days ahead, all twelve tribes of the nation (7:1–8). The second half focuses on the place and events taking place in Jerusalem in the south of the country (11:8, 'where their Lord was crucified') and at Armageddon in the north (16:16). It is not simply for nostalgic reasons that the metropolitan capital of the new universe is called after the Jewish capital. After all, its stones are inscribed with twenty-four Jewish names and not one Gentile. And it was Abraham who so looked forward to living in this city, that he was content with a tent, even in his old age (Hebrews 11:9–10).

CIRCUMSTANTIAL EVIDENCE

So far, in this chapter on 'the land', we have limited the discussion to relevant scriptures, the obvious priority for evangelical Christians. Nevertheless, conclusions of careful exegesis can be confirmed by events in real life. Archaeological discoveries that underline the accuracy of the biblical record are welcomed. Historical facts can likewise supplement confidence in God's word.

Christian Zionists would not be honest if they did not admit that their understanding of God's sovereignty over history and the unfulfilled prophecies has been influenced or at least enlightened by current events over the twentieth and twenty-first centuries. They come into the category of 'circumstantial evidence', which always has a cumulative effect. In court, a series of coincidental circumstances can be presented, none of which is in itself conclusive proof but all of which together, in the absence of any other evidence, can add up to a case 'beyond reasonable doubt'.

For example, a man is on trial for murdering his wife by pushing her over a cliff, beneath which her body was found. No-one saw him do it, so there was no eyewitness testimony and the case rested entirely on circumstantial evidence.

Among other facts, it emerged that he and his wife were in a bad relationship, constantly quarreling and fighting; that he had a mistress and had already booked flights for them both to Las Vegas and made inquiries about marriage licences there; that his wife was a Catholic and had refused a divorce; that just a week before the tragedy he had taken out a substantial insurance policy on her life. All of this, and particularly the last item, convinced the jury of his action, though unseen by anyone.

A series of extraordinary circumstances, taken together, has confirmed for many Christian Zionists that God was involved in the rebirth of the State of Israel, even though this was not visibly witnessed.

The first of these is their survival as an identifiable people through two millennia, exposed to the twin perils of assimilation and extermination. In spite of losing their country, language, coinage and so many other things that make up a people's self-consciousness, they retained just a few items in their culture (circumcision, Sabbath observance, and kosher diet) and, above all, a long memory of their history, kept alive by festivals like Passover and Tabernacles. Their survival contrasts sharply with the extinction of so many empires of their day as a nation. Where are the Assyrians, the Egyptians and the Babylonians today? Submerged in the Arab world, lost except for the ruins they left behind for archaeology. But Israel has survived and is back on the map. All this could be explained away by sheer dogged determination to be different from others, but God had promised not to let them disappear, as long as nature runs her course (Jeremiah 31:35–36). Coincidence or providence?

The second is the astonishing reversal of their 'fortunes' in just a few years, within one decade, the 1940s. From being the victims of the most barbaric horror of systematic genocide to becoming free citizens in their own country is unprecedented in human history. That the newly declared state was recognised within law by a majority vote in the United Nations was astonishing enough but surpassed by the fact that America and Russia for once voted together, though Russia later supported Israel's enemies. Britain, having relinquished responsibility for the Palestine Mandate, abstained from voting.

Israel's survival since 1948 is as amazing as her survival through the centuries of her Diaspora. Though not as spectacular or newsworthy as the 'Six Day War' later, the War of Independence immediately following the establishment of the state was even more startling. Grossly outnumbered and out-weaponed by an alliance of Arab nations determined to drive the fledgling state into the sea, they not only survived but would build up the sixth largest army in the world, with nuclear weapons in reserve. (Is this why the world's sympathy has so quickly transferred to the Arab cause, forgetting that there was an equal number of Jewish as Palestinian refugees in 1948, about half a million each?)

Israel has virtually been in a state of war ever since her establishment among the nations, with only temporary intervals of cessation of hostilities between attacks. Even during these pauses she has had to cope with more subtle forms of aggression, currently airborne missiles and suicide bombers. If the latter had killed the same proportion of the British population, we would be mourning 25,000 casualties.

Yet they have survived. This can be explained in terms of their determination, even desperation, knowing that their enemies can afford to lose many wars but they cannot afford to lose one. This author was taken up to the Golan Heights, in a jeep driven by an Israeli major, right at the close of the Six Day War. I stood near the Syrian gun sights and looked down the steep escarpment to the *kibbutzim* way below and could hardly believe such an apparently impregnable position had been captured by the Israeli forces. When I asked the major how it was possible, he answered silently by pointing to the sky. I believed him.

Many have commented on the undeniable contrast between the dry and barren landscape occupied by the Turks, barely able to support its meagre population, and the fertile and fruitful land today, supporting millions of Jewish and Arab immigrants. It can be attributed to the effort and ingenuity of Jewish farmers and their recently acquired agricultural skills, but there is one factor that clearly points to supernatural aid.

I was reading the history of Jewish *aliya* and came across a fascinating clue. When the first major group (in the 1870s) landed on the shores, there was a sudden and unexpected downpour of rain. A rabbi among them, with rain streaming down his beard, praised the God of Israel for this 'sign' of his blessing on their return. Was he theologically correct to do so? I determined to find out.

My wife's brother happened to be a professional meteorologist, first for the Royal Air Force and later on Midlands television. I asked him if he could get hold of any rainfall records for Palestine from the mid-eighteenth to the mid-twentieth centuries. He could and did. I transferred the figures to a graph and to my utter astonishment found that I was drawing a political graph as well! Apart from the fact that rain had increased over the whole period to two and a half times its original level, it had not done so evenly, but in steps, corresponding to the waves of Jewish immigration! When this eased off, notably during British restrictions, the figures remained steady or even fell back. And the highest rainfall for a hundred years was in 1948.

Alas, I must disappoint readers who want a copy of my chart. It is somewhere in my patent filing system. I never thought I would ever write about it and so far have not been able to lay my hands on it. So you will either have to take my word for it or do your own research. Some sceptics told me it was all due to a change in the micro-climate, brought about by the millions of trees planted on the hills. But this programme of forestation only got under way after 1948. For me it clinched the argument from circumstantial evidence.

Throughout the biblical history of Israel, rain had been a sign of his blessing brought by a western, moisture-laden wind from the Mediterranean, and drought a sign of his curse, brought by an eastern, hot and dry wind from the Arabian desert (the dreaded *hamsin*). Most have heard of the 3.5 years of drought in Elijah's day, and its ending when the prophet had decisively challenged the prophets of Ba'al (1 Kings 17–18). Many have been so used to interpreting the blessing (and ignoring the curse!) in Malachi (3:9–10) that they miss the meaning of 'open the windows [NIV has 'floodgates'] of heaven and pour out so much blessing . . . .' If God is still the Holy One of Israel, Israel is still 'his people' (Romans 11:1) and the land is still theirs (Romans 11:29), then it makes scriptural sense that he would look after their most urgent need, water, without which they would be unable to stay in the land.

To summarise this chapter, the combination of divine sovereignty over history, unfulfilled prophecies in scripture and circumstantial evidence from history and geography, have convinced Christian Zionists that neither the people nor their land have lost their significance to God.

As a footnote, we may add a comment on the fact that Sizer seizes on verses in the Old Testament that instruct Israel to deal generously with aliens ('strangers') within their territory and uses them to criticise the State of Israel today in her treatment of Israeli and Palestinian Arabs. I wonder if he realises that in doing this he is virtually acknowledging that these strictures only apply when the Israelites occupy the land that is rightfully theirs. Enough said.

5

THE SECOND COMING

All Christians agree that our Lord Jesus Christ is coming back again to earth from heaven, or at the very least say they believe he will whenever they recite a traditional creed. But that is where their agreement begins and ends. So many and deep are their disagreements about everything else but the basic fact that many Christians have stopped talking or even thinking about it. A concern for Christian unity has produced a kind of 'gentleman's agreement' not to discuss such things in polite ecumenical society, lest Christians divide over what many now consider a 'secondary' issue of little practical value, in which opinions are optional and convictions are offensive.

The result is that the Lord's return has slipped a long way down from its position in the Bible, where it is mentioned over 300 times. There are few contemporary worship songs about it. (One rare example envisages his second advent as a baby in a manger!) In a word, we have replaced an eschatological faith focused on the future with an existential love focused on the present. And hope is now the weakest of the three cardinal virtues, the casualty of a generation living for the here and now.

What has all this to do with Zionism? Well, for one thing,

all Zionists are very eschatological, quite out of keeping with current trends, both inside and outside the church. They think and talk a great deal about 'the Second Coming'. Most if not all of them take what is called the 'pre-millennial' position, which puts them at odds with the 'a-millennial' majority and the 'post-millennial' minority in the United Kingdom (we shall explain these terms later).

There is a clear connection between eschatology (belief about the end times) and attitudes to modern Israel. Our views on one affect our views on the other and vice-versa. They are inevitably interlinked.

I have already said (in chapter 1) that dispensational Zionists have made that link far too strong. In thinking of the Jewish return as the only sign needed of Jesus' *imminent* return to 'rapture' the saints, they have fostered an unhealthy and speculative expectation which could lead to disappointment and disillusion. While the New Testament hints that a Jewish return is a necessary prerequisite for Jesus' return, it nowhere states that this is a 'sign' of his impending arrival.

So what do 'classical' Zionists think about the Second Coming and how does that differ from 'covenantal' anti-Zionists like Sizer? Perhaps the simplest way to answer that is to work through some simple queries about Jesus' return, namely: how, where, when and, above all, why?

HOW WILL HE RETURN?
Sizer lists 'six things we can be sure of' — that his return will be personal, visible, unmistakable, sudden, unexpected and glorious. Some of these need to be qualified. For example, it will only be unexpected to unbelievers and sleepy believers (1 Thessalonians 5:1–8). Likewise 'sudden' implies with no previous warning; those watching for the 'signs' Jesus gave us will be fully aware of his approach.

But the real significance of Sizer's list lies in its omissions. He does not mention that he will be accompanied, either by angels or departed saints, thus emptying heaven of many of its inhabitants.

Far more important is that he avoids any adjectives which would indicate a physical return, what the early church called his 'corporeal' (i.e. bodily) return. Taking quite literally the angelic prediction at his ascension that 'this *same* Jesus . . . will come back in the *same* way you have seen him go' (Acts 1:11), it is no presumption to assume he will return not just 'with' but 'in' his resurrection body, which was able to be handled, could eat fish and cook breakfast. Why does Sizer not add 'tangible' to visible and 'physical' to personal? There are two possible explanations, one general, not directly relating to Israel, and the other particular, very much relating to Israel.

The general one is that 'Saint' Augustine, bishop of Hippo in North Africa in the fifth century, in his later ministry re-interpreted the Christian faith in a framework of Greek philosophy, which downgraded the physical and upgraded the spiritual, and has been a major influence on the Western Church, both Catholic and Protestant. This anti-physical prejudice led to a negative attitude toward sex (celibacy is more 'holy'), the afterlife (immortality of the soul replaced the resurrection of the body, and the new earth sank out of view) and other doctrines, all a denial of the Creator of matter. In relation to the Second Coming, it became much harder to imagine a physical Jesus returning to a physical world.

The particular reason may well be that returning with a physical body means returning to one place on earth. Even in his resurrection body, Jesus could not be in two places at once, though he could move swiftly from one to another (Luke 24:33–36). But he still had to 'go', from Judea to Galilee (Mark 16:7). All of which raises the next question:

WHERE WILL HE RETURN?
Since he will return in the same *way* as he went back to heaven (Acts 1:11), will it be to the same *place*? Both Old and New

Testaments seem to agree on this point: Jerusalem and its environs (Zechariah 14:4; Matthew 23:39).

Some time ago the Evangelical Alliance arranged a seminar on Israel in London and were surprised at the large attendance. Unfortunately, they fell into the same trap of assuming that there are only two positions and therefore invited only two speakers, the anti-Zionist Stephen Sizer and the dispensationalist Zionist Tony Pierce. The rest of us were limited to one question each. I asked Sizer where he believed Jesus was coming back to. I cannot recall his exact words but his answer was both vague and evasive.

It would have to be. Once you accept that his return will be physical as well as personal, tangible as well as visible, in a word 'bodily', then another adjective has to be added: it will be 'local'. Once that has been said, the location needs to be identified. I have never heard anyone claim it will be Rome or Geneva, Canterbury or Moscow. Every opinion that I have come across plumps for Jerusalem.

But that raises real problems for the anti-Zionist. It is one of their basic axioms that the land of Israel and its capital city have long since ceased to have any significance for the Lord, even if he still has plans for the Jewish people. The question: 'Why on earth would Jesus return to Jerusalem of all places?' becomes a real embarrassment. The only possible answer is that the place as well as the people is still integral to his purposes.

Is this why Sizer and others carefully avoid any language which would imply a physical location of Jesus' return? The omission speaks louder than words.

WHEN WILL HE RETURN?
The most basic answer is: only God knows. No humans know, no angels know, not even Jesus the Son of God knows (Matthew 24:36). The Father has fixed the date in his diary, but it is not for us to know (cf. Acts 1:7).

It is therefore unwise speculation when Christians guess what year it will be. Even great Christians have made attempts to work it out. Both Luther and Wesley ventured suggestions but were sensible enough to put it long after they would die, so they never had to eat humble pie! A number of contemporary sects have been founded on estimated dates (1914 for the Jehovah's Witnesses) but have had to explain away the mistakes with unimpressive rationalism. All such surmises so far have proved to be erroneous.

But that does not mean that Christians will have no idea at all, no signs to watch for, no warnings of his approach. We have already dismissed the dispensational teaching to this effect, the 'imminent', any-moment, any day now theory (I cannot call it 'theology' because I do not believe it is biblical).

Anti-Zionists and classical Zionists seem to agree that Jesus gave us 'signs' of his coming (notably in the 'apocalyptic' chapters: Matthew 14, Mark 13 and Luke 21). Sizer lists some of these (at first with tongue in cheek to show 'how easy it is to play games with the biblical text' but later more seriously). Then he makes the quite extraordinary claim that these 'signs' are of no use whatever to indicate the *timing* of the Second Coming! He argues this by claiming that the signs have been present for two millennia, ever since the first coming (wars, earthquakes, etc.) and that any biblical political events, particularly in the Middle East, have already been fulfilled in the fall of Jerusalem in AD 70 and do not await any further fulfilment in the future.

To say the least, this seems a rather strange and even misleading answer to the straight question of the disciples: 'what will be the sign of your coming and of the end of the age?' (Matthew 24:3, NIV). It makes Jesus' answer to be: 'No special signs will signal either event.'

This is to ignore the *sequence* of these 'signs', climaxing in the total eclipse of sun, moon and stars in the celestial sphere, after specific events in the terrestrial. There appears to be an intensification, perhaps an acceleration, of the latter, even in the world of nature, towards 'the end of the age'.

Zionists therefore conclude that the 'signs' are indicative of the timing of his return. They believe that alert Christians, watching and praying, will have first an approximate and then an increasingly accurate awareness that 'he is at the door' (Matthew 24:33). What keeps them from extreme excitement or even panic is the simple fact that by no means all the 'signs' are clearly visible yet (for example, universal hatred and persecution of Christians, Matthew 24:9), though the increasing speed of changes in world affairs could affect that quite quickly.

WHY WILL HE RETURN?
This question includes a number of subsidiary ones. What did he leave undone on his first visit that requires his return? How long will he need to stay this time? Why does he need to bring back with him so many already in heaven?

For many ordinary believers the simple answer (based on John 14:3) is that he is coming back to take us to heaven, or at least any of us still on earth at that time. But that would only take a few minutes and hardly needs his physical presence. We could be taken up like Enoch and Elijah and meet the Lord up in heaven. It all seems logistically unnecessary, especially if he brings with him 'those who have fallen asleep in him' (1 Thessalonians 4:14), millions of them, only to return them all later. Why hold the grand reunion down here rather than up there?

Surely he must have something to do on earth that requires his physical presence as well as all his people. Other texts make it clear that it is when he comes back that they will receive their new bodies, like his glorious body, whether their old ones have long since gone back to the dust from which they were made (and will be raised first) or are still breathing (changed in the blink of an eye). Bodies are not needed for life in heaven, but they are needed for life on earth, an indication that all Christians will be part of what Jesus is coming back to do. But what is it?

Traditional creeds say that it is to hold the 'Day of Judgement', for the whole human race, 'the quick (living and moving) and the dead'. That day will certainly come and Jesus will be the one seated on the 'great white throne' (Matthew 25:31; Acts 17:31; Revelation 20:11). But that last text adds that the judgement, based on written records, will take place *after* the universe, heaven and earth, have disappeared and there is 'no place for them'. So that cannot be the reason for his return to earth, unless he is coming to banish the earth first before getting on with the judgement.

We have reached the biggest difference between Zionists on one side, including both dispensational and classical, with anti-Zionists and a vast number of non-Zionists (with no views on Israel) on the other. Pretty well all Zionists believe Jesus is coming back to *reign* over the nations of this world for a lengthy but limited period before the universe passes away and the final judgement takes place. 'Loud voices in heaven' will announce that 'the kingdom of the world has become the kingdom of our Lord and of his Christ' (Revelation 11:15). He will obviously need the help of those he has redeemed with his own blood 'from every tribe and people and nation . . . and they will reign on the earth' (Revelation 5:9–10). Some will 'take charge of ten cities' (Luke 19:17).

I have quoted these texts because many think that the only basis for this belief in an earthly reign of Christ is Revelation 20:1–6. But that is a key passage and needs to be carefully examined and interpreted.

Few disagree with its basic message that Jesus and his 'blessed and holy' people will reign for a prolonged period. But there all agreement ends. Radically different answers are given to the crucial questions where and when will this 'rule' be.

First, where? Revelation is unique to the New Testament in moving from earth to heaven (e.g. 4:1) and back again more than once. So the context of each 'scene' of the drama is important. Chapter 20 is clearly set on earth ('out of heaven' in verse 1, 'the earth' in verses 8 and 9, etc.). The reign is on earth, not in heaven.

Second, when? It may seem rather trite to point out that chapter 20 follows chapter 19 and precedes chapter 21 but common sense assumes that there is a chronological sequence here, that the reign of Christ and his saints will come after his return to earth but before the new heaven and earth. Another characteristic of the whole book reinforces this conclusion. There are so many sevens in it. Seven golden lampstands and seven stars (chapter 1), seven letters to seven churches, each with seven parts (chapters 2–3), seven spirits of God, with seven horns and seven eyes (chapters 4–5), seven seals (chapters 6–7), seven trumpets (chapters 8–9), seven bowls of wrath (chapters 15–16). But there is a final seven, which goes unnoticed by many readers, partly because it is spread over three chapters. Chapter divisions were never part of God's inspired Word, and were made by a bishop centuries after the 'canon' (rule, standard) of scripture was closed, often putting asunder what God had joined together (note the divisions between Genesis 1 and 2, Isaiah 52 and 53, Acts 18 and 19). Read the final chapters of Revelation straight through without pausing over the chapter numbers and the continuity is readily seen. Another feature of the whole book reveals the final 'seven', the divine revelation coming alternately verbally (in voices heard) and visually (in visions seen). 19:10 ends a section of 'heard', which is resumed in 21:3. In between are a number of 'and I saw' visions, which reveal seven events:

i. Jesus' return — on a white horse of war (19:11–16);
ii. 'Battle' of Armageddon—prequel and aftermath (19:17–21);
iii. Incarceration of Satan (20:1–3);

iv. Reign of Christ and his saints (20:4–6);

v. Release of Satan and final 'battle', Gog and Magog (20:7–10);

vi. Day of judgement (20:11–15);

vii. New heaven and earth — new Jerusalem (21:1–2).

That these events are intended to be read as a chronological sequence is clear from the text itself (for example, 20:10 refers back to 19:20 as having already happened). Almost all Bible scholars accept the sequence of Second Coming, day of judgement, new heaven and earth. But too many remove everything in between the first two of these and insert them somewhere else in the calendar, quite arbitrarily, as we shall see. At the very least, they should acknowledge that the series of visions came to John in a chronological sequence!

To believe the visions indicate a chronological sequence of events is to take the '*pre*-millennial' position, that is that Jesus will return *before* the reign over earth with his saints, hence the prefix 'pre-'! It is unfortunate that this has become so associated with dispensationalism. All dispensationals are pre-millennial, but by no means all pre-millennials are dispensational. Such records as we have suggest the church of the first few centuries was pre-millennial, believing Jesus would return for a 'corporeal [bodily] reign on the earth' (Papias, Bishop of Hierapolis), centuries before any hint of dispensation.

Pre-millennials take Revelation 20:1–10 in its simplest, most straightforward sense, believing the whole book was written for ordinary Christians and not in an obscure code only understood by experts. That does not mean they take the whole of Revelation literally. No-one does. All recognise there is symbolism in it. Some symbols are obvious, some explained (the dragon is the devil), some are paralleled and explained elsewhere in scripture, leaving only a few which still puzzle us (usually because we are so far from the original readers in time, place and culture). But context indicates where the text is symbolic. It is as mistaken to say everything is symbolic as to say that nothing is. And behind every symbol is a fact which is being symbolised. So the whole of Revelation is pointing to facts and needs to be interpreted factually.

Classical Zionists take it as fact that Jesus will return to earth, to make war with the leaders and forces who have suppressed and persecuted his people, to defeat them in a 'mother of all battles' that is not really a battle at all (he will slay them with his tongue, as he once killed a fig tree); that the devil will be rendered utterly helpless, while Jesus and his saints rule the world in righteousness 'for a thousand years', but Satan will be released for his final deception and damnation. (Few notice that there is more information here about Satan's destiny than that of the saints!)

The phrase 'a thousand years' is taken literally, in the absence of any indication that it should not be. After all, it is mentioned six times, twice with the definite article. How often does God have to say something before we take him seriously? Even those who take it symbolically agree it means an extended period of time.

The word 'resurrection' is taken literally. Always this noun is applied to the body. The word 'first' is taken literally, meaning there will be two resurrections, one at the beginning of the 'millennium' for the 'holy' and the other at the end for the 'rest of the dead' (the former is variously referred to in the rest of the New Testament as 'the resurrection of the righteous' [Luke 14:14] or 'the resurrection *out* from (among) the dead' [Philippians 3:11].) Incidentally, verse 10 is also taken literally to prove that hell is a place of perpetual torment, first for the two human agents of Satan, the Antichrist and the false prophet, then for Satan himself, and later for those whose names are not still found in the book of life (20:15; cf. 3:5 and 21:7–8, the last references clearly referring to believers failing to overcome). This was the curse of 'everlasting punishment' pronounced by Jesus himself (Matthew 25:41). Annihilationists, please note.

This then is the 'pre-millennial' position, taking literally what seem to be presented as facts. How else would the original readers, ordinary Christians in the south-east of what is now Turkey, have taken them? Why then are Christians today so divided? What has changed?

Quite simply, the first ten 'verses' of 'chapter' 20 have been taken out of their context, out of the sequence of visions and therefore out of the sequence of events. The 'millennium' is then inserted into the history of the church *before* the Lord's return, which is then described as '*post*-millennial'. That is, Jesus returns *after* the millennium. Technically speaking, there are only two basic positions, the 'pre-' and the 'post-', with their completely contradictory answers to the question: when will he come?

But there has been a further sub-division among the post-millennials, introducing a third label into the debate. It would have been more accurate to use the same noun for both of these (for both transfer the millennium to the period before the Second Coming) and separate adjectives to indicate a secondary difference. I shall do this, but indicate how and why the different names arose. Both groups claim Augustine's book *City of God* as their source. He was the first post-millennialist, but was somewhat ambiguous in his application.

What I will call the '*political* post-millennialists' take the 'thousand years' literally and apply the phrase to the final phase of church history before Christ returns. By then the world will have been 'Christianised', not that everyone will have been converted but Christians will have grown in sufficient numbers to take over all governments. The kingdom of God will thus have been established on earth by the church, as a *fait accompli* to present to the King of kings on his return, though it will have been achieved in his name and by the power of his Spirit.

Of course this means that Jesus cannot return for at least another thousand years and probably very much more than that, since we are nowhere near taking over, even after two thousand years. So those who think this way hardly think about his return, much less preach it.

Many missionary hymns of the late nineteenth and early twentieth centuries reflected this optimism, from the days when the British Empire was growing and spreading both the faith and Western civilisation alongside each other. Two world wars were a serious setback to such optimism and 'post-millennialism' of this kind. But it has had a fleeting revival in recent years, under the titles of 'restorationism' in the UK and 'reconstructionism' in the US.

The programme has no room for the revival of Israel as a nation. The British magazine *Restoration*, after a successful run, devoted an entire issue to anti-Zionism — and went out of circulation shortly afterwards.

But there is another group, which I call the '*spiritual* postmillennialists'. They take the 'thousand years' symbolic-ally and apply it to the whole of church history between the first and second advents of Christ. Since this has already been two thousand years, the 'thousand years' have to be taken metaphorically, as do many of its descriptive details. The reign of Christ has to be in heaven rather than on earth and the saints who share it are divided between those already in heaven (the church triumphant) and those still on earth (the church militant), though the co-ordination of the two is something of a mystery. The reign is demonstrated on earth in the church and by the church in any situation where Satan is defeated. While political influence may be expected, political dominance is not envisaged.

There will be no reign of Christ on earth after his return. The day of judgement and creation of the new heaven and earth will follow immediately. The physical restoration of 'Israel', either people or place, has no part in the scheme of things, though some allow for a spiritual revival among the Jews, sweeping many into the church before the end (based on

Romans 11:26). All post-millennials share a negative attitude towards the modern State of Israel.

How do 'spiritual' post-millennialists distinguish themselves from the 'political' sort? They have left the politicals with the label 'post-millennial', even though they are also 'post-', and coined a new label for themselves: 'a-millennial'. This is a misleading misnomer, since the prefix 'a-' denies whatever it is attached to, as in 'atheist', someone who denies the existence of God (*theos* in Greek). 'A-millennials' don't deny the millennium. In fact, they believe we are already in it!

However, this raises real problems when it comes to applying Revelation 20 to the present. We have already noted that it involves a radical revision of the chronology. Chapter '20' is believed to mark the beginning of a digression, in fact a 'flashback' in time, describing a period *before* the events described in chapter 19. But that is only the beginning of the following re-interpretations of the descriptions of the millennial events:

i. The angel who deals with the devil ceases to be a created servant of God, as everywhere else in this book and indeed the whole New Testament, and becomes the Creator Son of God, Jesus himself, who 'bound' Satan on his first visit to earth, either at the beginning of his ministry (Matthew 12:29) or at the end (John 12:31).

ii. The five words describing what happens to the devil, (chained, bound, thrown, locked, sealed) are reduced to one, 'bound', ignoring the others. One that would cover them all is 'banished', since it is clear that he is totally cut off from his former sphere of influence, the world, quite unable to continue his deceptive activities. But if a-millennials believe this has already happened, as they do, how do they explain the New Testament teaching that 'he prowls the earth like a roaring lion looking for prey to devour'? By denying that he is locked and sealed in the 'Abyss' (the lower depths of the earth) and postulating a very long chain that allows him to reach anywhere in the world! 'To keep him from deceiving the nations anymore' is reduced to 'can't stop the gospel spreading and releasing his subjects'.

iii. 'The first resurrection' is not of bodies at all, only souls, and refers to individuals 'raised from the death of sin' (Ephesians 2:1). It thus happens every day, not on one day. The second is a resurrection of bodies, all on the same day. This distinction between them means that the phrase 'come to life' has an entirely different meaning in verse 4 to verse 5.

We could go on but we have said enough to show how a-millennials treat Revelation 20. Apparently nothing means what it says and we need theologians to explain it to us. Pity the original readers, who seemingly took it all at face value, judging by the views of the early church. I leave the readers to judge for themselves whether the above 'explanations' are really interpretation or manipulation of the text to fit a pre-conceived conclusion.

I have gone into this question thoroughly because Sizer does. I believe all Christians need to be informed about the debate and come to their own conclusions and convictions. The different views have profound effects on attitudes to Israel today. The majority of evangelical Anglicans, for example, would probably call themselves 'a-millennial', after the major Protestant Reformers, Luther and Calvin, which could explain the widespread ignorance and indifference concerning Israel.

At the grass roots level, an increasing number are taking refuge from the controversy under the label 'pan-millennial', explained as a simple confidence that 'everything will pan out alright in the end anyway', implying 'why bother about it now?' But this flippant quip virtually consigns Revelation 20 to the waste paper basket at worst or the 'pending tray' at best. Those who do this need to be reminded of the terrible consequence of losing a place in God's future blessings (22:19).

Sizer does not clearly align himself with any position, though reading between the lines suggests that he inclines to the typical Anglican a-millennial position. However, he mentions sympathetically a fourth position, which he calls 'preterist'. If 'pre-' puts the millennium in the future *after* Jesus' return, 'post-' puts it in the future *before* the return and 'a-' puts it in the present. This 'fourth' puts it into the past, all having been fulfilled in the first generation after Jesus' first coming! This novel and recent contribution achieves nothing but more confusion, to my mind. By introducing it, does Sizer hope to make the debate so complex as to discourage it altogether?

While he does not make clear which view he himself espouses, he makes abundantly clear which one he does not — the pre-millennial. His criticism of this is severe. He seems unaware that it was held by the early church but very aware that it is held by most Zionists, particularly the main target of his polemics, the dispensationalists. His major accusation is that pre-millennials are supremely 'pessimistic' about the immediate future. I agree that they hold an 'apocalyptic' philosophy of history, which may be simply summarised in a two-fold statement — things will get much worse before they get better, but they will get much better after they get worse.

That statement is a good working outline of the contents of the book of Revelation as well as books of prophets in the Old Testament. It could be claimed to summarise the biblical philosophy of history, pessimistic about the immediate future, optimistic about the ultimate future. It is neatly encapsulated in Jesus' parable of the wheat and the tares. Good and evil, the works of God and Satan, will both grow towards maturity with increasing competition and confrontation between the two, until the tension is resolved by supernatural intervention. On this basis, I believe pre-millennials are being realistic rather than pessimistic. Certainly they do not share the optimism of the post-millennial expectation that the church will take over the world, nor the optimism of the a-millennials that things will get no worse than they are now and even a bit better. It is interesting to note that the mood of society shifted radically from optimism at the beginning of the twentieth century ('progress' was the big word) to pessimism at its end. This mood has carried over into the twenty-first century ('survival' is the big word). Few today would defend the idea that the world is getting better and better. In health and wealth, for some, yes. For peace and happiness, for many, no. The gap between rich and poor is widening. Billions are spent on space exploration and weapons of destruction while millions starve. Are pre-millennials utterly mistaken to pin their hopes on the return of Jesus to reign over the world with peace and righteousness, bringing multilateral disarmament and world peace (or is Isaiah 2:4 yet another Old Testament prophecy that must not be taken literally?)

Hope, along with faith and love, is a vital dimension of Christian living. It is an 'anchor for the soul' (Hebrews 6:19). But an anchor is no use while displayed on the deck, however strong an impression it gives. It must be out of sight, geared to solid reality to hold the ship against tide and storm. Christian hope cannot rest on the shifting sands of human speculation but must cling to the solid rock of divine revelation. We 'wait for the blessed hope — the glorious appearing of our great God and Saviour, Jesus Christ' (Titus 2:13, NIV).

Note:

For a much more detailed discussion of the issues raised in this chapter, see the author's *When Jesus Returns* (Hodder and Stoughton) and the final section of *Unlocking the Bible* — Omnibus edition (Harper Collins).

CONCLUSION

THE CONSEQUENCES

Supposing that I am wrong! This thought has haunted me as I have written these pages, as it does every time I put pen to paper. Some leading Zionists and many others have told me I was the one who opened their eyes to the significance of Israel. Even Stephen Sizer blames me for his earlier Zionism, now abandoned. Though my recorded messages on the subject are less than 2% of all my available material, they seem to have had an influence out of all proportion. Indeed, at one stage, when people began to call me 'the Israel man', I pulled away from speaking about Israel for quite some time, wanting to be known as a teacher of 'the whole counsel of God' (Acts 20:27).

To have misled so many trusting Christians would be a fearful burden on my conscience, knowing that all teachers in the body of Christ 'will be judged more strictly' (James 3:1). I can only beg readers not to believe anything I have written until they have 'searched the scriptures' (not just looked up textual references) as the Bereans did to check out Paul himself (Acts 17:11). I have often concluded a talk by saying: 'If you can't find all this for yourself in your own Bible, forget it, for God's sake.' I mean it. It is my safety net!

This story of how I changed from a tourist in Israel to a convinced Zionist is told in my autobiography (*Not as Bad as the Truth*). A series of amazing adventures in the land and with the people undoubtedly had an influence and could be dismissed as subjective and even sentimental. That is why I have kept anecdotal material out of this volume and concentrated on scriptural data, hopefully in an objective way that can be easily verified.

I think I am ready to face the appalling consequences if I am wrong.

But suppose that I am right! Then I have raised the prospect of serious consequences for others. Israel would cease to be an optional interest for some Christians, a kind of hobby that can become a hobby horse. Israel would be of vital concern to all Christians, intimately involved in their future destiny.

If the Abrahamic covenant is still in operation, as I have claimed, then the people of Israel still belong to the Lord and the land still belongs to them. Furthermore, one vital provision of that covenant still applies — 'I will bless those who bless you, and whoever curses you, I will curse' (Genesis 12:3). Coming immediately after 'I will make you a great nation', it seems clear that 'you' refers to the nation and not just those who bless or curse Abraham himself.

All too frequently today, a sentimental rather than a scriptural view of God expects him ever to bless but never to curse. But both Testaments witness to the latter (the last word of Elijah in the Old, Malachi 4:6, and the last word of Jesus to the 'goats' in the New, Matthew 25:41).

Is there any historical evidence for the operation of this covenantal principle? I believe there is, even in my own life-time. I begin with examples of nations that betrayed God's chosen people.

Germany immediately springs to mind. After their defeat in World War I, Hitler gave the nation a recovered hope and pride. He made the third attempt to build a 'Reich' (kingdom, empire), claiming it would last 'a thousand years' (his ersatz substitute for the biblical 'millennium'!) Yet in less than twenty it was reduced to smouldering rubble, following his suicide. He is probably most widely remembered today for his barbaric extermination of six million innocent Jews. Was it merely a coincidence that Germany's defeat and downfall began in the same year as the 'Final Solution' to the 'Jewish problem' was put into action?

What about Britain? In abandoning the Jews in Palestine to what many expected to be their extermination at the hands of the surrounding Arab nations, our nation was betraying a trust given to her by the inter-war League of Nations and breaking her word to the Jewish people to secure a homeland in their ancestral territory. Full details of this disloyalty can be seen in a DVD *The Forsaken Promise* (produced by the Hatikvah Film Trust and directed by Hugh Kitson, who also told me my teaching awoke his interest in Israel). Don't watch if you don't want to be embarrassed or even ashamed to be British. In just a few years, after 1947, the British empire had disintegrated. It had once included a third of the world's population, circled the globe ('the empire on which the sun never set'); but it was rapidly reduced to a handful of seaports and tiny islands. Another coincidence? Or was God saying: 'If you can't look after my people, you can't look after any'?

The story of British Prime Ministers is striking. One after another has disappeared from the political scene after letting God's ancient people down. The list includes Neville Chamberlain (and the infamous White Paper of 1939 severely restricting Jewish immigration to Palestine when they most needed it), Anthony Eden (and the Suez fiasco), James Callaghan (I am not at liberty to give details of his broken promise, but he lost a vote of confidence a few days later). The most spectacular example was Winston Churchill. After a lifetime of Zionist support, he turned against the Jews in the late spring of 1945, weeks before losing the first post-war election. He wrote a stinging letter to Chaim Weizmann (as we noted, the man who had saved Britain in World War I by discovering how to make acetone, a vital ingredient for explosives, from wood pulp). It seemed that Churchill blamed the whole Jewish people for the assassination of his friend

Lord Moyne in Cairo, by Irgun, a Jewish resistance movement.

On the other hand, the three Prime Ministers who held office for the longest time over the same period were all staunch Zionists: Harold Wilson, whose major publication *The Chariots of Israel* is largely unknown; Margaret Thatcher, who was a member of the 'Conservative Friends of Israel' and who supported our meeting in Finchley marquee when I spoke about the debt Gentiles owe to the Jews; and Tony Blair, who inaugurated the annual Day of Remembrance each January to remind us of the horrors of the Holocaust.

I had the opportunity to speak on these 'coincidences', both negative and positive, to an invited group of Members of Parliament, from both sides of the House of Commons, meeting in the Speaker's apartments, at the invitation of George Thomas, later Lord Tonypandy. I was congratulated on my courage, but it is simply that I am more afraid of upsetting God than people.

If all this is evidence of the God of Israel's activity in the political sphere, what about the ecclesiastical? Many factors could explain the Church's steady decline in numbers and influence. Compromise in both belief and behaviour have clearly reduced respect and confidence in the general public, though local fellowships maintaining traditional/biblical doctrine and ethics still appeal. But they are the exception, not the rule. Mainline denominations are reporting losses or at best just maintaining their statistics. 'Christian' England is a thing of the past.

Now a rising tide of anti-Zionism is added to the mix. The Archbishop of Canterbury consents to speak at a conference in Jerusalem, sponsored by the Palestinian Liberation Theology Centre and specifically denouncing Christian Zionism, though it must be added that the mildness of Rowan Williams' contribution surprised and disappointed the sponsors. The most belligerent speaker died shortly after returning home. Stephen Sizer was a delegate. Some preachers deliberately attack Israel. More promote support for the Palestinian cause. Perhaps most simply ignore the Zionist challenge, considering it an irrelevant distraction from the real business of church.

How does the Holy One of Israel feel about all this? One telling indication is the biblical description of Israel as 'the apple of his eye' (Deuteronomy 32:10; Zechariah 2:8). Though this phrase has entered the English language, few appreciate its meaning. People think of a child's eyes lighting up when given a rosy red apple to eat. But it refers to the eyeball itself and the iris in particular, which resembles an apple viewed from the stalk side, with its radiating stripes. It is the most sensitive spot in the whole human body, protected by the eyelid, which immediately slams down when the slightest alien particle threatens its welfare. When God is described as the 'keeper' of Israel, the Hebrew word for 'eyelid' is used, highlighting his extreme sensitivity when they are touched in a hurtful way. This also applies to his people called Christians (Matthew 25:31–46), who are also 'God's chosen people' (Colossians 3:12); but it still includes the Jews (as we have seen in chapter 3).

As is usually the case, the real issue is theological rather than ethical or even political. Not whether we believe in God, but what kind of God we really believe in. There are aspects of his character which explain his attitudes and actions, but which are being ignored or neglected in so much contemporary preaching. One obvious example is his jealousy. When did you last hear a sermon on his jealousy for his name (his reputation) and his people? Then there is his righteousness, which explains why he blesses some and curses others, heals some and kills others, loves some and hates others. His feelings about us are far more important than our feelings about him. What makes him happy or sad, contented or angry? When was the last time you heard his wrath explained, its causes and its effects on individuals and society? (Read Romans 1 for evidence that he is angry with Britain now).

A hedonistic generation does not want to hear about such things so we offer a 'user-friendly' Christianity, whose gospel is summed up in three words: 'God loves you', which neither Jesus nor the apostles ever preached (see my books: *Is John 3:16 the Gospel?* and *The God and the Gospel of Righteousness*).

Above all, God's moral integrity is at stake, his reliability, his faithfulness. Does he stand by his word? Does he keep his promises? Does he mean what he says and say what he means? We have seen that the New Testament itself points out that if he goes back on his promises to Abraham, our new covenant hope becomes insecure (Hebrew 6:13–19).

I conclude this defence of Christian Zionism by asking the reader two simple yet profound questions:

First, do you trust God? This reliable, trustworthy God who makes covenant promises and keeps them. This God who is not a man that he should change his mind.

Second, do you fear God? Because he is so consistent, so just, so absolutely fair, judging everyone impartially, with no favourites, above all bribery and corruption. One of the most frequently quoted texts in the Bible is, 'The fear of the LORD is the beginning of wisdom' (Proverbs 1:7), but few who quote it realise that 'LORD' in capital letters is the English substitute for the Hebrew name for God (JHVH, pronounced 'Yahweh'), given to them by God himself. So our final question becomes: Do you fear the God of Israel? I do.

APPENDIX
John Stott's Sermon

In allowing Stephen Sizer to include one of his unpublished sermons, John Stott is not only lending his name but implying his approval of the general thrust of Sizer's thesis. Indeed, there is little difference between their attitudes to Israel.

The most obvious is the difference in tone. Stott's writing seems the more reasonable. However, this does not hide the fact of their fundamental agreement in content.

Stott's use of the name 'Israel' says it all. Admitting that 'in olden days "Israel" was a physical designation, meaning the descendants of Jacob', he claims that, 'today "Israel" is a spiritual designation, meaning believers in Jesus, whether they are descendants from Jacob or not.' This, of course, is the basic tenet of all replacement theology.

Ignoring over seventy references to 'Israel' in the New Testament, all of which are clearly ethnic in meaning, he focuses on the one and only possible exception (Galatians 6:16), which can be applied to the church by substituting the word 'even' for 'and'. It is unlike such a careful scholar to build so much on so flimsy a foundation.

His conclusion is that 'true Israel' is made up of 'neither Jews nor Israelis' but the people of Jesus, believers in the Messiah.

Nevertheless, he does acknowledge the continuing existence of what he calls 'physical Israel', alongside the 'true spiritual Israel'. Nor does he seem embarrassed to call them both 'Israel'. And he believes that God has a 'special' future for physical Israel. Unlike Sizer, with many if not most biblical scholars, he takes 'Israel' in Romans 11:26 in an ethnic sense, as it certainly means in 11:25 and throughout the chapter. He rightly looks forward to 'a widespread turning of Jews to Christ'.

But — and it is a big but — this 'special future' is entirely spiritual and not in any way physical. The land once promised to them is utterly irrelevant. God's plans for them as a people require their continued existence and identity but their location is a matter of indifference. Their return to their ancestral home has no theological or biblical significance whatever.

Like other anti-Zionists he points out that Old Testament prophecies link a return to the land with a return to the Lord, adding that it is hard to see how the secular State of Israel can be seen as a fulfilment. He ignores one feature of those prophecies, that the return to the Lord would follow the return to the land; and one fact, that since 1948 the number of Israelis believing in Jesus has rocketed from a few dozen to tens of thousands (and this has happened in the Diaspora as well over the same period).

Stott says: 'I leave aside political considerations' and promptly proceeds to include them! He adds, by way of 'example', that he is excluding 'the grave injustices that have been done to the Palestinians and the risk of further Israeli expansion'. No mention of Palestinian missiles or suicide bombers.

In one of his video recordings Stott called Jesus 'a Palestinian'. Apart from being an anachronism (the name Palestine had never been heard of then), it is a highly emotive thing to say in the contemporary conflict and could even mislead young untaught converts into thinking our Lord was an Arab. I had hoped it was a mere slip of the tongue, but now I am not so sure.

However, Stott does condemn all anti-Semitism, confessing that the Christian church has been responsible for much of it. Like Sizer, he sees anti-Zionism as something quite different.

He also freely acknowledges the debt Christians owe to the Jews (the scriptures, the apostles, our Saviour himself).

When it comes to expounding particular texts Stott gets into difficulties, coming up with some unusual, even bizarre, explanations.

Luke 21:24, taken at face value, is a prediction of Jesus about the future of the city of Jerusalem, that it will one day be liberated from assault and occupation by Gentile forces and become again the Jewish capital. For Stott, 'Jerusalem' does not refer to the Jewish capital at all but to 'the whole present world order', which will be brought to an end before Jesus returns. This extraordinary claim is all of a piece with his understanding that the Antichrist and the false prophet are not persons but social forces.

While on Revelation, he interprets the multitude in 7:9 as 'the fullness of the Jews and the fullness of the Gentiles', while ignoring the first six verses of that chapter which speak of the protection and preservation of the twelve tribes of ethnic Israel at the same time.

He accepts that God has not rejected Israel (Romans 11:1) then immediately adds that 'God's rejection of them' is not final!

But these are mere quibbles. Perhaps the heart of Stott's position is his statement that, 'the New Testament writers apply to Christ both the promises of the seed and the promise of land (i.e. made to Israel through the patriarchs Abraham, Isaac and Jacob)'. He can refer to Galatians 3 for the seed but significantly gives no references for identifying Christ with the 'land'. There aren't any.

He does not comment on Romans 11:29, which categorically states that the gifts of God to the patriarchs are 'irrevocable'. Foremost among these was the promised land.

In summary, it is a great pity that this sermon had not remained unpublished but has been used to bolster Sizer's blistering attack on Christian Zionists.

Unlocking the Bible
is also available in DVD format from
www.davidpawson.com